S0-EIA-930

PR
3069
·I69
G48
2008

87589

SHAKESPEARE, PERSIA, AND THE EAST

BY
CYRUS GHANI

CONCORDIA COLLEGE LIBRARY
BRONXVILLE, NY 10708

MAGE PUBLISHERS

Copyright © 2008 Cyrus Ghani

Cover painting is of Sir Robert Shirley [Sherley] (1581?-1628)
by Sir Anthony van Dyck,
Petworth House, The Egremont Collection
(acquired in lieu of tax by H.M.Treasury in 1957 and subsequently
transferred to The National Trust),
©NTPL/Derrick E. Witty

All rights reserved.
No part of this book may be reproduced
or retransmitted in any manner whatsoever,
except in the form of a review, without the
written permission of the publisher.

Library of Congress Cataloging-in-Publication Data

Ghani, Sirus.
Shakespeare, Persia, and the East / by Cyrus Ghani.
p. cm.
Includes bibliographical references and index.
ISBN 1-933823-24-0 (alk. paper)
1. Shakespeare, William, 1564–1616--Knowledge--Iran.
2. Shakespeare, William, 1564–1616--Knowledge--Orient.
3. Shakespeare, William, 1564–1616--Friends and associates.
4. Great Britain--Relations--Iran.
5. Iran--Relations--Great Britain. I. Title.
PR3069.I69G48 2008
822.3'3--dc22

2008009827

First hardcover edition
ISBN 1-933823-24-0
ISBN 13: 978-1-933823-24-9

Printed and manufactured in U.S.A.

MAGE BOOKS ARE AVAILABLE AT BOOKSTORES,
THROUGH THE INTERNET
OR DIRECTLY FROM THE PUBLISHER:
MAGE PUBLISHERS, 1032-29TH STREET NW
WASHINGTON, DC 20007
202-342-1642 • AS@MAGE.COM • 800-962-0922
VISIT MAGE ONLINE AT
WWW.MAGE.COM

This small effort is dedicated
to my young granddaughters, Laila
the fifth grade "Juliet" and Roya her
"Romeo" for practicing lines.

∞And

To the memory of dear friends
Alireza Arouzi and Mehran Tavakoli
who died too soon to see its publication.

CONTENTS

ACKNOWLEDGMENTS

In my studies of Shakespeare I was very fortunate in having had several excellent teachers to whom I owe a great debt of gratitude. They were Virgil Markham, son of a well-known poet, Edwin Markham, at Wagner College; Alfred Harbage and William Nelson at Columbia University; and Francis Ferguson at the New School for Social Research.

Over the years I had amassed a collection of some six hundred books on Shakespeare and his works, which I have given as a gift to Bard College, my late son's alma mater. I am indebted to Jeff Katz and Debra Pemstein of the Stevenson Library of Bard College for having returned to me on loan a number of those books to assist in research for this work.

I want to thank Paul Sprachman of Rutgers University, friend and erstwhile collaborator on an earlier project, for providing me with lists of translations of Shakespeare in several Eastern languages. Encouragement came from many sources, but I am most grateful to my friend Hasan Kamshad formerly of Cambridge University who also offered assistance by sending me several books of Persian translations of Shakespeare's plays. Ahmad Mahdavi Damghani who has taught at various universities and is now visiting professor at Harvard assisted with his knowledge of Persian poetry. I was given support and confidence by Alinaghi Alikhani and the late Arthur Schlesinger, Jr. As always, my friend and publisher Mohammad Batmanglij had an important role in offering valuable advice.

Most of all I owe a great deal to my wife Caroline who was also a student of English literature and like myself a law school graduate. She assisted me beyond measure almost to the point of coauthorship. She endured my doubts, my demands, and my moods. She knows how much I appreciate it.

INTRODUCTION

Books about Shakespeare and his work abound. His plays have been translated into almost all known languages. His every word has been analyzed and interpreted. There are numerous books and articles dealing with Shakespeare's interests ranging from food and flowers to music and even medicine. The present volume is yet another such study concerning Shakespeare's knowledge and interest in Persia, as well as other Eastern areas. Shakespeare was sufficiently schooled in history to provide him with references to ancient Persia. As a child of the Renaissance, it was a part of his body of knowledge. There were also books and pamphlets written about Persia of later years by travelers, which most probably came to Shakespeare's attention.

Shakespeare was very much a man of his time. His daily concerns were providing for his family, financial security, and public recognition. His interests included local chatter and rumors making the rounds in the Globe Theater, in the Mermaid Tavern, and on the streets of London. They also concerned court intrigue and political activities, which all enriched his plays. He surely was aware that other lands and cultures were of general interest at a time of wide-ranging exploratory ventures and commercial enterprises.

Persia was of substantial interest to England and other European countries of the sixteenth and seventeenth centuries as they shared a common adversary, the Turks of the Ottoman Empire who had made conquests and inroads in eastern Europe, eventually as far as the gates of Vienna. There were efforts by leading European countries and by the Pope to encourage Persia to wage war against the Ottomans thus diverting them from making further advances in Europe. There existed enmity between the Ottomans and the Safavid monarchs who had declared Persia a Shi'a state, which the neighboring Sunni Turks regarded as a heresy and a mortal threat. The major European military powers promised to simultaneously wage war. Despite their encouragement and assurances it appears that the Europeans had no intention or lacked the will and resources to take part in the conflict. They were content to have the Persians keep the Ottomans engaged. During the entire Safavid era there was not one coordinated campaign with Persia against the Ottomans.

How Shakespeare came by his interest in and knowledge of contemporary Persia is a prime focus of this study. It attempts to place Shakespeare's knowledge in its historical context. In this regard, the Earl of Essex and the Sherley brothers play prominent roles as well as Southampton, Shakespeare's patron and a disciple of Essex. In addition to Essex's military escapades, he was interested in commerce. What is relevant to the subject of this book is Essex's sponsorship of the Sherley brothers' travels to Persia. Their mission was to convince the Persians to mount a campaign against the Turks and also to assess trade and commercial possibilities between England and Persia. The Sherleys became known personalities in London and the public followed their adventures.

Shakespeare was writing for the average theater audience and while some of his classical allusions may have eluded them, contemporary references would more likely have been recognized. Shakespeare brought to his audiences names, locales, and stories from the East concerning diverse times and places, some familiar, some not so well known, but all designed for the interest and entertainment of the public.

In the course of this study the names Persia and Iran are used interchangeably as it suits the context. The language is uniformly referred to as Persian.

Iranians refer to their country as "Iran." The Greeks, rivals of Iran in eastern Mediterranean lands, referred to the same geographical entity as Persia. Europeans thereafter followed the Greek example, as, of course, did Shakespeare. In any case, Persia was a misnomer as it referred only to the province of Pars (Fars). This was the province of Alexander the Great's seat at Persepolis after his conquest of Iran.

According to the *Avesta,* the holy book of the Zoroastrians, the pre-Islamic indigenous religion, Iran was one of the seven countries of the world. It is referred to as Iranshahr. In ancient times Iran as a country was the heart of the Persian Empire.

The first recorded historical reference to the name Iran is by King Hormozd of the Sasanian dynasty in A.D. 271 in an inscription that reads "I am the king of Iran and Turan." Some scholars believe that the terms Iran and Turan do not refer to a geographical entity but to a people, Iran designating believers and Turan nonbelievers.

The first recorded mention of Iran as a country in the Islamic era is in the poetry of Rudaki Samarqandi (d. A.D. 954). A century later Iran appears numerous times in the poetry of the epic poet Ferdowsi (932/4–1020). By the mid-Safavid era in the late sixteenth century the country is uniformly referred to as Iran.[1]

---

1. Dr Jalal Khaleqi Motlaq, "Iran in the Pre-Islamic Era," *Iran Shenasi*, fourth year, no. 2 (Summer 1992): 240–1. Dr. Jalal Matini, "Iran in the Islamic Era," *Iran Shenasi*, fourth year, no. 2 (Summer 1992): 243–98.

A BRIEF BIOGRAPHY OF
WILLIAM SHAKESPEARE

"He was not of an age but for all time."

Ben Jonson
Preface to *First Folio*, 1623

S hakespeare was born on 23 April 1564, some five
years after Elizabeth's coronation. Elizabeth's England was a small place not to be compared with the
great contemporary civilizations: Ming China, Moghul India, Safavid Iran, or Ottoman Turkey whose
combined territory stretched from China to south-
eastern Europe. England was an island off the edge of
Europe with a population of less than three million.
But within a century the center of gravity shifted from

the old civilizations of Asia to the maritime states of the Atlantic seaboard.

Notwithstanding the surfacing of eccentric conspiracy theories about the life and works of William Shakespeare, there are no mysteries about his life. We know more about him than any writer of his time. His grandfather, father, mother, birth, marriage, children, and death are all on public record. We have the date and place of his baptism and his last will and testament. We have records of his many business transactions, contracts, and documents involving him as principal or a party of interest. His name appears numerous times in the recorded journals and letters of his contemporaries: Robert Greene, Henry Chettle, Francis Meres, John Davis, Ben Jonson and the editors of the *First Folio,* and fellow actors, John Heminges and Henry Condell.

Shakespeare's mother and father both came from farming stock – old families rooted in the Warwickshire countryside. Definite knowledge of William Shakespeare's family begins with his grandparents Richard and Margaret Shakespeare.[1] Richard

---

1. The origin of the name Shakespeare is "one who holds the spear." Some early ancestor may have distinguished himself for military prowess. It is possible that the family name came from across the channel during the rule of English kings in northern France, the first syllable deriving from *sac,* which means to draw out vigorously, and the second from an earlier spelling of *épée*, a dueling sword. John Quincy Adams, *A Life of William Shakespeare* (U.S., 1925).

was a farmer from the village of Snitterfield about four miles from Stratford-on-Avon. Richard died in 1561. He had two sons, John and Henry. John, the elder, married Mary Arden, the daughter of a family of landowners. By all accounts she was a formidable figure, respected by neighbors. There are records of John having prospered for a time as a glover and dealer in wool. By 1552 John Shakespeare had moved to a large house in Stratford that stands today and is named "The Birthplace" of his son William. On 22 or 23 April 1564 William was baptized. In 1566 another son Gilbert was born and in 1569 a daughter Joan. In 1574 and 1580 two sons were born respectively named Richard and Edward. Only Joan outlived her brother William. In 1568 John was elected high bailiff of Stratford. From 1577 there was a decline in John's fortunes owing probably in part to the decline of Stratford as a center of the wool trade. By 1576 John had been dropped from the list of aldermen. Several biographers believe that his reverses had something to do with prevalent rumors of his retained Catholicism. Like others in England the Shakespeare family went through the traumatic experience of having to change their church of worship from Catholic to the Church of England established by Henry VIII. In the first ten to fifteen years of Elizabeth's reign there had been a degree of tolerance for adherents of the "old religion" as long as they did not publicize their Catholicism. In April 1566 the queen appointed a commission to enquire into offences against the monarch. In 1576 the

Statute of Supremacy had made the monarch, not the pope, the supreme head of the Church of England. Those who willfully absented themselves from church services were to be fined for their transgression. Anyone who held civil office now had to take part in the act of allegiance to the queen in all matters related to religion. Investigations were held throughout the land in 1576, which coincides with John Shakespeare's last appearance at a Stratford town meeting.

In due course young William went to grammar school. From about 1571 he attended what was known locally as the "Big School." In the Tudor era most subjects were taught in Latin, the language of the church and the law. Shakespeare was probably introduced to the comedies of Plautus, which later inspired his own plays, one being *The Comedy of Errors*. Shakespeare also read the plays of the Roman dramatist Seneca and it is nearly certain that he became acquainted with Ovid. There are references to Ovid's work in several of his plays (e.g., *Titus Andronicus*[2]). William never went to university; possibly the worsening financial condition of his father did not allow it.

In November 1582 William married Anne Hathaway, the daughter of Richard Hathaway, a large landowner and a neighbor. When they married, William was eighteen and she twenty-six. As their first child

---

2. Titus: Lucius, what book is that she tosseth so? / Boy: Grandsire, 'tis Ovid's Metamorphoses, my mother gave it to me. (IV, 1, 43).

was born some five months later it has been assumed by several biographers that the marriage was forced. Some maintain that it was an unhappy marriage, especially since after the birth of twins Shakespeare spent considerable time away from Stratford. Anne and William had three children. The first born was Susana in 1583. On 25 February 1585 twins were christened in Holy Trinity Church in Stratford. They were named after their neighbors Hamnet and Judith Saddler who presumably became the godparents. On 11 August 1596 Hamnet died by drowning at age eleven. Some scholars believe that it was a defining moment in Shakespeare's life. Changes began to come about in Shakespeare and in the themes of his plays, their language, and imagery. Shakespeare's father died in 1601, his mother in 1605.

Between William Shakespeare's marriage in 1582 and his definitive mention in the London theatre the only documented record of his whereabouts is the baptism of his children and a court case of 1587. Most probably Shakespeare left Stratford for London in the late 1580s. It has also been speculated that from some time near that date Shakespeare had begun working as an actor in a professional theatrical company in or around the Stratford area. A few have argued that Shakespeare stayed in Stratford and wrote poetry. It is only from about 1591 that we can say with a degree of certainty that he was in London as an actor and probably working on his first comedies.

By the early 1570s professional theatre had begun to gain respectability. Before then acting companies were itinerant, performing at any suitable location: large halls, town squares and even open fields. After the performances a hat or wooden bowl was passed. By the late 1570s professional theatre groups started to attract the sponsorship of the wealthy and aristocrats. A few small permanent theatres were built. Sponsors of the troupes included the Lord Admiral or the Lord Chamberlain. It has been estimated that in the mid-1590s there were about 3,000 spectators per week. Another influence in the growth and popularity of theatre was Queen Elizabeth who enjoyed the theatre and often held performances at court. The principal restrictions on plays being staged were: the text had to be reviewed by authorities; no performances could be held on religious holidays; and all plays were to be licensed by the Lord Mayor. The Queen's Men were one of the leading acting troupes. It had been founded in the 1580s by Sir Francis Walsingham (the spymaster). His troupe was under instruction by the court to spread Protestantism and loyalty to the queen, and to identify any seditious group. The Queen's Men were to play an important part in Shakespeare's initiation into the theatre and playwriting. Also among the established groups were the Lord Strange's Men, the Essex Men, and other smaller groups.

Shakespeare arrived in London at the time when the dramas of Thomas Kyd and Christopher Marlowe were drawing large numbers of spectators. The success of *The Spanish Tragedy* by Kyd in 1586 appears to have been the primary inspiration for Christopher Marlowe to write another play of bombastic eloquence, *Tamburlaine*, an epic about the son of an eastern Asian shepherd who became king of "half the world." *Tamburlaine* had its first performance in 1587 and established Marlowe as a dramatist of great talent. He was the first dramatist to regard himself as a poet. Thereafter the most important element in his plays was language and not mere spectacle. He was one of the first playwrights to use blank verse, which freed and revolutionized English theatre.[3] Marlowe soon became the favorite of theatre audiences. His downfall was related to his association with people of questionable character and to his blasphemous views. He ridiculed the religious order, the church, and people of authority. Marlowe died in 1593 at age twenty-nine, stabbed by Ingram Frizer, one of his companions.

Most of the playwrights of the day came from the same or humbler social stations than Shakespeare: Thomas Kyd was the son of a London scrivener, Christopher Marlowe was the son of a shoemaker in Canterbury but had been fortunate enough to attend university, as were Robert Greene the son of a saddler

---

3. Blank verse: The unrhymed iambic pentameter of English dramatic and epic poetry that Shakespeare perfected. For example: "What light is light if Sylvia be not seen / What joy is joy if Sylvia be not by." *Two Gentlemen of Verona* (III, 2, 174–5).

and Thomas Nash the son of a curate. Neither Shakespeare nor Kyd had been to university. As products of only grammar schools both were spoken of condescendingly by the university-educated for their lack of formal learning.

Shakespeare was fortunate in having chosen to become a playwright at a time of expansion of English urban society, the English theatre, and the English language by the borrowing and even inventing of new words. The Queen's Men's rhyming verses gave way to the new blank verse, which had great appeal.

In February 1593 to June 1594 theaters were closed due to an outbreak of the plague. It was only possible to perform plays at court or at the homes of noblemen outside of London. Shakespeare had to seek other means of support. The closing of the theaters placed financial pressures on him. He had to care for his family in Stratford in addition to his own expenses in London. Patronage could provide income and a degree of social advancement. He looked toward the Earl of Southampton, a young man of wealth who was fond of the theater.

Henry Wriothesley (pronounced Riseley), Third Earl of Southampton (1573–1624), was some nine and a half years younger than Shakespeare. He came from an old prominent Catholic family with estates in Hampshire at Titchfield and Beaulieu. His grandfather Viscount Montague had served Henry VIII and his father had been Lord Chancellor.[4] Southampton's father had been one of the notable Catholics who had not submitted to the Protestant faith. Southampton was eight when his father died in 1581. There were rumors that he died under mysterious circumstances. The great Lord Treasurer Burleigh, a friend of Southampton's father, became his guardian. At age twelve he was sent to St. John's College, Cambridge. He was then entered in Gray's Inn as a "gentleman of means and birth" and completed his education in law. Southampton fell under the mystique of the dashing Earl of Essex who was to play an increasingly important role in his life.

With the closing of public theaters Shakespeare selected to seek the patronage of the young earl who had already acquired a reputation as a devotee of poetry. In addition the Earl of Southampton was an avid theatergoer and Shakespeare was regarded as a playwright of great promise.

Shakespeare dedicated one of his longer poems *Venus and Adonis*[5] to Southampton. The dedication reads in part: "Right Honourable, I know not how I shall offend in dedicating my unpolished lines to your Lordship…" Some thirteen months later Shakespeare

---

4. Southampton could count the famed John of Gaunt among his own ancestors.

5. *Venus and Adonis* was probably written in late 1592. It was entered in the Stationer's Register on 18 April 1593.

dedicated another poem, *The Rape of Lucrece*,[6] to Southampton. The second dedication reads in part "... what I have done is yours, what I hope to do is yours being part of all I hope." Shakespeare appears to have been on respectfully familiar terms with his patron. This is more evident in the emotional dedication of his second poem. Shakespeare was fortunate in gaining Southampton's patronage. We have no record of the nature of the assistance Southampton offered Shakespeare, but undoubtedly he showed his appreciation with some financial reward.

Shakespeare soon became the most popular playwright of his time. One of the elements that made him popular was his feel for the speech of ordinary people and the ability to communicate with the audience. In the explosion of the English language Shakespeare introduced many new words and usages that have immeasurably enriched the language. Shakespeare also became a master of the new and popular blank verse form. Another element was his fondness for England of bygone years. Falstaff, probably his most endearing character, is of that era and he became a favorite of theatergoers after the staging of the two *Henry IV* plays. Shakespeare's plays on the Hundred Years War with France brought back memories of England's victories at Agincourt and Crécy and the hero king Henry V. Still another element in the popularity of Shakespeare was that unlike the majority of Englishmen of

6. *The Rape of Lucrece* was registered on 9 May 1594.

his time he was tolerant of both the old and new faiths as reflected in the tone of his comedies. He was born to a Catholic family but perhaps abandoned his family's religion over the years.

By 1597 Shakespeare had achieved some material success and acquired a large house in Stratford. He was in Stratford in 1607 when his older daughter Susana married Dr. John Hall. Although Dr. Hall was somewhat of a puritan there is evidence that Shakespeare got along well with him. Shakespeare's other daughter Judith married a local hatter in 1609 of whom very little is known. There is a record of Shakespeare's younger brother Gilbert having died in Stratford in 1612.

There was a second outbreak of the plague and theatres were closed between 1608 and 1609. Shakespeare continued writing but at a slower pace. Between 1611 and 1612 he wrote his last play *The Tempest* in which he prepares us for his retirement:

Prospero: I'll break my staff
Bury it certain fathoms in the earth
And deeper than did ever plummet sound
I'll drown my book.
V, 1, 54–57

In his last years we have records of Shakespeare having bought more property in Stratford. He prepared a draft of his last will dated 25 March 1616 and died on 23 April of that year. His last direct descendant was his granddaughter Elizabeth Hall, Susana's daughter, who died in 1670.

Between 1591–92 and 1611 Shakespeare had written thirty-seven or thirty-eight plays (one in collaboration), more than 150 sonnets, two lengthy narrative poems, and some short poems. He is recognized as the greatest master of the English language and his canon of works is equal if not superior to any great works of literature. He stands high in the pantheon of literary immortals alongside Dante, Goethe, and the Persian poet Hafez. His works have been accorded a place in Western culture beyond other writers. They can be classed as humanistic scriptures.

THE TUDORS 1485–1603 AND THE SAFAVIDS 1495–1720

THE TUDORS

HENRY VII 1485–1509

The Tudor dynasty began with Henry Tudor of Richmond (1457–1509). The Tudors descended from a small Anglesey family with connections to English, French, and Welsh royal houses. Henry's grandfather Owen Tudor had secretly married Catherine de Valois, widow of Henry V, and when Henry VI came to the throne the Tudors were in favor and were treated deferentially. Through his mother his claim to the throne was even more substantial as his great-great-grandfather was the legendary John of Gaunt. Henry VII was the only son of Edmund Tudor, Earl of Richmond. He spent the first fourteen years of his life in

South Wales and was always conscious of his Welsh ancestry and obligations. The Welsh in turn supported the Lancastrians in the War of the Roses. Thus from the outset Henry had been a potential threat to the Yorkist monarchs and there had been attempts to do away with him.

The reigning king Richard III (1452–85) was the son of the Duke of York. He was made Duke of Gloucester by his brother Edward IV and distinguished himself in the War of the Roses. On Edward IV's death in 1483 Richard was appointed protector to his nephew Edward V but soon secured the crown for himself maintaining that Edward IV's sons were illegitimate. Most historians maintain that Richard III was cruel and had murdered Edward V and his brothers. In any event these suspicions made Richard unpopular. Meanwhile Henry Tudor bided his time. He soon raised an army and in 1485 faced Richard's forces at Bosworth. Richard was killed in battle and Henry ascended the throne as Henry VII.

The War of the Roses and the ceaseless battles that had raged during the reigns of Henry VI and Richard III finally came to an end. Henry was crowned in Westminster Abbey and he effected a permanent peace thereafter by the union of the "Roses." Henry VII of the Red Rose of Lancaster married Elizabeth the heiress of the House of York, the White Rose. The marriage established the legitimacy of the Tudors. Henry died in April 1509 at age fifty-two.[1]

The Tudor dynasty consisted of three generations: Henry VII, Henry VIII (1509–47); his son Edward VI (1549–53); and his daughters Mary (1553–58) and Elizabeth (1558–1603). The House of Tudor lasted for nearly 120 years and within two generations England became the dominant power in Europe.

HENRY VIII 1509–47

Henry VII and Elizabeth of York had three sons and four daughters, though only their second son, the future Henry VIII, and their two eldest daughters, Margaret and Mary, were to survive their parents. Henry VIII came to the throne on a wave of popularity. He had received a good general education. He knew Latin and some French, and was interested in theological discourse. He held lavish banquets, dances, and tournaments as he had inherited a full treasury. He had a good principal advisor and chancellor, Cardinal Wolsey, who held power until 1529.

On his deathbed Henry VII had advised his son, the future Henry VIII, to marry Catherine of Aragon, daughter of King Ferdinand and Queen Isabella of Spain. She was the widow of his eldest son Prince

---

1. Shakespeare devotes nine plays to the War of the Roses and successive kings: *Henry VI, parts 1, 2,* and *3*; *Richard II*; *Richard III*; *Henry IV, parts 1* and *2*; *Henry V*; and *Henry VIII*.

Arthur who had died at age sixteen shortly after the marriage. Henry VII had emphasized that Prince Henry's marriage to Catherine was important to preserve the Spanish alliance. Following his father's advice Henry married Catherine. He was overjoyed when on New Year's Day 1511 Catherine gave birth to a son, but the child only lived six weeks. Thereafter there was a series of miscarriages, but in 1516 Queen Catherine gave birth to the healthy Princess Mary (known later as Queen Bloody Mary). It became clear, however, that Catherine would bear no more children. Henry began to think that his marriage was unfruitful because it was against God's law as Catherine had been the wife of his older brother.

Henry appealed to the pope. He argued that Catherine had never been his lawful wife as she had been married to his brother. He also argued that he wanted a son born in wedlock who could ultimately succeed to his throne unchallenged. Pope Clement VII refused to rule. Then Lord Chancellor Cardinal Wolsey argued that Henry's marriage was void ab initio and therefore the king could marry again. The pope again refused to rule. In this interim Henry became infatuated with Anne Boleyn, the daughter of courtier Sir Thomas Boleyn. Henry assumed that he could marry her since Wolsey was having negotiations with the pope.

Others were advising Henry that he must withdraw all allegiance to the pope in order for him to be legally free of Catherine. Catholic zeal was at its lowest ebb when Henry struck at the Church of Rome. He had parliament proclaim him head of the new Church of England. He had several churchmen executed for having dared to deny him this status.

Henry secretly married Anne Boleyn in January 1533 following Archbishop Cranmer's ruling that Henry's marriage to Catherine had been null and void. Anne was crowned queen at Westminster Abbey when she was apparently already pregnant. She gave birth in September 1533 to Princess Elizabeth. Henry was not entirely happy as he had wanted a male child.

Before long Anne was accused of adultery. There was some circumstantial evidence. She was tried, found guilty, and executed on 19 May 1536. Henry then married Jane Seymour on 30 May 1536. She bore him a son, Edward, the male heir Henry always had wanted. Jane died shortly after giving birth. The search for an alliance with a Protestant state influenced Henry's selection of his next wife, Anne of Cleves, daughter of the German Duke of Cleves, who spoke no English and could not be considered attractive. An anullment was soon arranged. Henry then married Catherine Howard. Henry's sixth and last marriage was to Catherine Parr whose previous two husbands had died. The last three marriages were without issue.

The passing of medieval England was greatly advanced by the demands of Henry VIII who was impatient to be divorced. His impatience provided the first tentative steps in the separation of church and state. Other elements also contributed to change: the growth of London and rise in population, the rise of an educated middle class, and the expansion of trade with European countries and Asia. By the beginning of the sixteenth century Europe had begun to form national states: France, Spain, and Portugal. Power became increasingly concentrated in the hands of monarchs. The power of the barons and dukes lessened. Henry VIII was one of the most important of English kings. Historians have emphasized that the growth of English democracy owes a great deal to the separation of church and state, which had its beginnings during his reign.

EDWARD VI 1547–53

Henry VIII's young son by Jane Seymour, Edward VI, ascended the throne in 1547 when he was ten years old at a time of intense political turmoil, exiles, and executions. Edward was more fervent and harsher than his father in his commitment to the eradication of the Catholic faith. He was pious, cold-hearted, and surrounded by a small group of politically motivated men. Now the destruction that had befallen monasteries fell on churches that were suspected of propagation of the old faith. The first version of the English Book of Common Prayer was written in 1549 during Edward's reign, as was the declaration that England was a Protestant state.

When Edward died in 1553 in his teens, his half-sister Mary, daughter of Catherine of Aragon and a devout Catholic, became queen.

MARY 1553–58

Mary was well received when she ascended the throne but soon lost all good will by her intolerance and wanton cruelty. She did her utmost to reverse her brother's religious revolution. She soon earned the sobriquet "Bloody Mary" by burning Protestants. In her drive to restore the Catholic faith in England she committed numerous atrocities in the name of God.

Mary's right to the throne was challenged by Lady Jane Grey, a grandniece of Henry VIII. She was proclaimed queen but was ousted within nine days by forces loyal to Mary. Mary then married the Catholic king Philip II of Spain, England's principal rival. The marriage was not successful. During her brief five year reign Mary failed in her principal mission to return England to Catholicism. Her cruelty united the English and intensified their hostility toward Rome and the Catholic church.

ELIZABETH 1558–1603

The Act of Succession had determined that after Henry VIII's death the crown would go successively to Edward, Mary, and then Elizabeth, his three surviving children. Elizabeth had been well tutored as a child. She had had a capable governess, had learned several languages, and was schooled in the classics and history. She had been badly treated during Edward's reign by the key powers behind the throne. Much worse, during Mary's reign she was in effect exiled and even had been confined briefly in the Tower of London fearing for her life.

Elizabeth ascended to the throne on 17 November 1558. Now at age twenty-five she had become queen and the people rejoiced after the excesses of Edward and Mary. On her accession she boasted to her close circle that she was English to the core. Her mother was no Spanish princess and her father was the founder of England's new church and the English navy. Elizabeth inherited traits from both parents. She was heir to her mother's vanity and her father's determination and resolute character.

Although she was not entirely forgiving of those subjects who had remained Catholics and refused to attend the services of the Church of England, she was a realist and devised a middle path attempting to placate the various factions. She had admired her father and his achievements both in matters of religion and state, but she realized the bringing together of a divided nation was her most urgent task.

As an unmarried queen she created an uncertainty. Her close advisors reminded her of advantages to her and to England of a suitable marriage. Parliament continued to press her to marry for reasons of stability and the issue of succession. But Elizabeth paid no heed. Proposals of marriage came from, amongst others, the king of Sweden's son and the Duke of Savoy. But Elizabeth was adamant and repeated that she had no desire to marry. The question of succession that had arisen after Mary's death was again brought forward by Elizabeth's cousin Mary Stuart, Queen of Scotland and wife of the Dauphin of France, claiming the crown should pass to her after Elizabeth's death. Since Mary Stuart was a fervent Catholic, Elizabeth and her advisors refused to even enter into such discussions. When Mary's husband who had become King Francis II of France died, Mary returned to Scotland and revived her claim as Elizabeth's rightful successor, which Elizabeth again dismissed. Later in 1586 Mary apparently joined in a plot whereby a certain Anthony Babington and his followers intended to assassinate Elizabeth. Mary was tried for treason and executed on 8 February 1587. There was fear that France with the support of Spain might invade England. But Spain was not yet ready. It would be a year later that Spain would mount an all-out campaign for the invasion of England with the Spanish Armada.

Although Elizabeth never married, she had her favorites. Several commentators believe Elizabeth may have married Lord Robert Dudley had he been unmarried. She had other favorites over the years: the Earl of Leicester, Sir Christopher Hatton, later Sir Walter Raleigh, and lastly the Earl of Essex with disastrous results. She dispensed favors among these men:

Raleigh was given monopolies in the import of tea and playing cards and in tavern licenses; Essex had a monopoly of sweet wines; other favorites had monopolies for the entry and exit of goods in English ports.

Elizabeth was fortunate in having trusted advisors who served her well throughout her reign. She placed exceptional trust in William Cecil (later Lord Burghly, High Treasurer). Cecil was an advocate of caution and moderation, but in critical times he would urge swift action. In 1560 he persuaded Elizabeth to send an army to Scotland to support the Reformation movement and he played a leading part in the events leading to the execution of Mary Queen of Scots. He advised Elizabeth to exercise caution to avoid a breach with Spain before England was prepared. Cecil employed Sir Francis Walsingham, a strong Protestant, who set up an elaborate intelligence system that proved crucial in uncovering plots by Mary Queen of Scots, and later the details of the impending attack by the Spanish Armada.

From the outset Elizabeth's most urgent problem was the religious schism. The English Reformation was a revolutionary step in which believers in the old and new faiths were victimized alternately. She avoided the excesses of Edward and Mary and created an environment for the factions to live together peacefully. Shakespeare who had been raised as a Catholic conformed and became the Queen's favorite playwright. Elizabeth is also noted in history for her cautious conduct of foreign affairs. Her success was in large part due to the emergence of England as a sea power, which changed the equilibrium in Europe and made England ascendant.

Neither the Phoenicians nor Romans in the pre-Christian era nor the Venetians at a later date had to traverse vast oceans. Ships only had to cross the Mediterranean Sea to reach the southern coasts of Spain and Portugal, then via Gibraltar to reach the southern ports of England, Flanders, and northern Germany. With the discovery of the American continent in 1492 by Spain the sea supremacy of the Italian city states became limited to the Mediterranean. Then came the discovery of a sea route to Asia around the Cape of Good Hope to the Indian Ocean by the Portuguese navigator Vasco da Gama in 1497–99. This gave Portugal a great advantage in the Persian Gulf and in commerce with India.

Spain and Portugal began to colonize the South American coast. When England's turn came some fifteen years later they had to be content with the colder climate of North America. France, the other power of Europe, attempted to follow the example of the earlier colonizers, but they were restrained by the sectarian conflicts at home between the Huguenots and Catholics. Europe was looking eastward for trade as well. England's interest in Persia was heightened as evidenced by travelers and the numerous references in Shakespeare's plays to the East in general and Persia in particular.

The father of England's navy was Henry VIII who had built a powerful fleet. Although neither Edward nor Mary improved it and even neglected its maintenance, nonetheless the navy inherited by Elizabeth was still the most modern in Europe. Although Spain fell behind as a naval power, it remained the most formidable military power in Europe. With the annexation of Portugal, Spain acquired the Portuguese possessions in the East. There was not much England could do. It asked for a sort of "open door" policy in the Americas and independence for the Netherlands, which Spain had occupied. Spain ignored the requests. Elizabeth's advisors, most notably Francis Walsingham, urged Elizabeth to oppose the forces of Counter Reformation everywhere in Europe, and to assist the Protestants in the Netherlands against Spain.

The Low Countries were part of the Hapsburg Empire. The Netherlands was a divided country. The southern provinces, mostly Catholics, looked to Spain to intervene and make the Netherlands a Spanish province. The Dutch under William the Silent, the head of the House of Orange that had turned Protestant, led a movement to expel the Spaniards and preserve the unity of the country. Spain managed to maintain the southern province, which is now Belgium. When William was assassinated in 1584, the Protestants turned to the queen of England for help.

Elizabeth did not want a war with Spain; however, her advisors urged intervention as standing aside would encourage Spain to take further drastic actions. Robert Dudley, the Earl of Leicester, was chosen to lead an expedition. Leicester was outmanned and could do nothing. Later the Earl of Essex commanded forces in the Netherlands. Not a great deal was accomplished by either mission against the very able Spanish general Parma.

Spain with the annexation of Portugal had become the dominant power in Europe. It upset the balance of power and the Counter-Reformation movement headed by Spain began to surface in other countries. Spain decided that it was not enough to isolate England and began thinking of its conquest. The consequence of England's turning toward the ocean, its intervention in the Netherlands, and repeated raids on Spanish ports was a war with Spain.

Philip II of Spain had devised a plan to be rid of its main rival. The plan was to send a large fleet across the English Channel and link with the army of the Duke of Parma. Spanish ships would destroy the English navy and Parma's army would land on the southern coast of England. The Spanish counted on the population to support the invasion as England was only a recent convert to Protestantism and some of her subjects had retained their old faith. Furthermore, Ireland was predominantly Catholic and the people had long harbored resentment against English rule. They would be encouraged to rise up against the English, which would tie up some of the English forces. The Spanish also believed that Elizabeth was unpopular for having had her cousin Mary Queen of Scots executed.

These assumptions did not meet expectations. The Irish uprising did not take place until the following decade. Fierce storms had destroyed nearly half of the Spanish ships on the Irish coast. The Spanish fleet had also missed the link-up with the Duke of Parma's army, the critical element for the Spanish. Parma was hemmed in by the Dutch and English and was unable to move. English naval technology had proved to be superior to that of the Spanish. The English ships were smaller but faster and more maneuverable. The Spanish Armada was defeated by an outnumbered English fleet. The defeat of the Spanish Armada established England as Europe's leading naval power. It was a defining moment of the Elizabethan era.

On 17 November 1588 bells rang out for the anniversary of the queen's accession to the throne but also to celebrate the defeat of the Spanish Armada. There was a surge in Elizabeth's popularity. The war between England and Spain continued until the death of Elizabeth in 1603 and the accession of James I, but, shielded by the sea, England was never invaded. This security was enjoyed by no country in Europe. As John of Gaunt says:

This fortress built by nature for herself
Against infection and the hand of war,
…
This precious stone set in the silver sea,
Which serves it in the office of a wall…

Richard II, II, 1, 43–47

THE SAFAVIDS

The Safavids, like the Tudors, brought unity and stability to their country. They also were responsible for
the spread of a new religious order. The difference,
however, was that Iran was not protected by a sea and
suffered many invasions in her long history.

A BRIEF OUTLINE OF EARLY IRANIAN HISTORY

Iranian recorded history begins with the advent of the
Achaemenid dynasty (550 to 330 B.C.). The Achae-
menids were probably a Persian-speaking nomadic
tribe that came through the Caucasus to the Iranian
Plateau. By the end of the sixth century B.C. they had
settled in the region of the present province of Fars.
They united with the Medes,[2] another regional tribe.
From a marriage between an Achaemenid and the
daughter of a Median ruler a son Cyrus was born, later known as Cyrus the Great. By maturity Cyrus had
defeated Croesus, king of Lydia, whose wealth was

---

2. Media is referred to in Shakespeare's *Antony and
Cleopatra* (see page 145).

legendary, and by 546 B.C. the Persian Empire was established. Cyrus then conquered Babylon which submitted peacefully and he freed the enslaved Jews from captivity. He is known in history as a benevolent ruler who respected local traditions and laws.[3] Cyrus brought artists and artisans from Babylon to create his palace and tomb at Pasargad.

On Cyrus's death in 529 B.C. there was discord between his sons Cambyses[4] and Smerdis, in which Cambyses prevailed and ascended the throne. Shortly thereafter Cambyses conquered Egypt. While there, a rebellion erupted in Iran and it is reputed that Cambyses took his own life. Other accounts have it that he was assassinated.

Darius, a new claimant, suppressed the rebellion and ascended the throne in 521 B.C. He reorganized his empire into Satrapies (provinces) with Satraps (governors) responsible to the king. He decreed Zoroastrianism as the state religion. Darius then conquered Thrace and Macedonia and all of Asia Minor. However, he was defeated at the battle of Marathon in 490 B.C. and withdrew from the Greek peninsula.

---

3. Cyrus the Great is prominently mentioned in the Old Testament in the books of Ezra and Isaiah. Cyrus and his descendants are also praised in the books of Nehemiah and Esther. Cyrus is referred to in Shakespeare's *Henry VI, Part I* (See page 117).

4. Cambyses is the subject of a play by Thomas Preston (circa 1570) titled *A Lamentable Tragedie Mixed Full of Pleasant Mirth Containing the Life of Cambyses the King of Persia*. Shakespeare refers to Cambyses in *Henry IV, Part I* (See page 125).

Darius's son Xerxes I (485–466 B.C.) was also defeated by the Greeks at Salamis and the Persian fleet was destroyed in 460 B.C.[5]

Soon thereafter there were revolts in Egypt and the Persian Empire shrank considerably in the ensuing years. There followed several inconsequential Achaemenid kings leading to the rule of Darius III[6] in 336 B.C. He was killed in battle against Alexander the Great's invading army in 330 B.C. The conquest of Persia having been completed, Alexander marched to its spring capital at Persepolis, which was capriciously set aflame. Alexander continued eastward to northwestern India and died on the return journey in 323 B.C.

The Achaemenid dynasty contributed considerably to world civilization. It produced two superior leaders, Cyrus the Great and Darius the Great, who were skilled administrators, particularly in the organization of their far-flung empire.[7] They created powerful art and architecture and a literature in cuneiform.

After Alexander's death, Iran was administered by his military leaders. Soon there was strife amongst

---

5. The defeat of the Persians at Salamis is the subject of the earliest known play *The Persians* by Aeschylus written in 472 B.C., some eight years after the event, which Shakespeare might well have read at school.

6. Darius III is referred to in *Henry VI, Part 1* (See page 119).

7. The motto of the Iranian mail service of the time as quoted by Herodotus is well known: "Neither snow nor rain nor heat nor gloom of night stays the couriers from the swift completion of their appointed rounds." It is engraved on many post office buildings in the United States.

them and Seleucus obtained possession of Alexander's Asian conquests. A few regions remained independent under Iranian Satraps. The Seleucid dynasty ruled over a fragmented Iran from circa 312 B.C., but within a few decades Seleucid rule became limited to northern Syria, Mesopotamia, and western Iran.

A new dynasty, the Parthians,[8] who came from northeast Iran, ruled several parts of the original Achaemenid Empire (circa 214 B.C.). In 188 B.C. the Romans conquered Greece and Macedonia and slowly progressed to western Asia. But their advance was halted by the defeat and death of their general Croesus in 53 B.C. by the Parthians, whose expert archers inflicted great casualties on the Roman armies.

The continuing warfare with the invading Romans weakened succeeding Parthian rulers and in A.D. 226 Ardeshir ascended the throne, founding the Sasanid dynasty. Ardeshir's principal objective was to restore the grandeur of the Achaemenid Empire and conquer the lost territories. He revived the Zoroastrian religion, which unified the country. In A.D. 260 Shapour I ascended the throne. One of his first accomplishments was the establishment of Jondi Shapour, an institution of higher learning. He then turned his efforts toward recovering the provinces lost to Rome. He invaded Roman dominions and took the Roman emperor

---

8. The Parthians and Parthia are prominently referred to in *Antony and Cleopatra* and also mentioned in *Cymbeline* (See pages 147, 153).

Valerian as prisoner of war. A temporary truce with Rome was established but was soon shattered. Hostilities continued for nearly three hundred years, rendering both Iran and Rome weak and vulnerable.

In A.D. 636 the Sasanids were defeated by Arab invaders at the battle of Qadisiyyah. The crucial defeat and surrender of Iran came some six years later at Nahavand. Major cities including former capitals at Ctesiphon and Susa fell to the invaders. Within ten years the Arab conquest was complete. Iran became merely a province of the Arab Empire where the center of power had been first Medina, then Damascus, and later Baghdad. In a relatively short time a sizable number of Iranians adopted Islam, the religion of the invaders. The Arabs were committed to the spread of Islam and within a brief span the Arab Empire stretched from Samarqand east to India and west to Arabia, the entire Middle East, North Africa, and parts of Spain.[9]

The first significant Iranian break with Arab rule came about with the rebellion led by Yaqub Ibn Laith, who then established the Saffarid dynasty in A.D. 867. Within some fifteen years he ruled in Herat, Turkestan, and Khorasan, as well as the province of Fars.

From the late tenth century, Mahmoud of Ghazna ruled all of northeast Iran. After intermittent wars with the Ghaznavids, the Seljuq Turks from central

---

9. Shakespeare refers to the Prophet Muhammad in *Henry VI, Part 1* (See page 118).

Asia controlled most of eastern, northern, and even a sizeable territory in western Iran. Although not ethnic Iranians, the Seljuqs adopted Iranian culture and traditions, and Persian became the language of the Seljuq court. The last of the Seljuq kings was defeated and overthrown by Changiz Khan in 1220.

Changiz Khan (circa 1160–1227) was born Temuchin, the son of a Mongol chieftain. He succeeded his father and assumed the title of Changiz Khan. He conquered all of China, Central Asia, and parts of northern India, and brutally swept across Iran. He then advanced to parts of eastern Europe as far as what is now Hungary. His conquests were marked by ruthless destruction.

Next to invade Iran was Teimur (Tamerlane) (1336–1405). He was born in Central Asia, probably Turkestan, the son of a tribal leader. He claimed descent from Changiz Khan. By 1369 he controlled all of Central Asia and made Samarqand his capital. He then conquered lands east of the Euphrates; in 1392 he conquered the entire area between the Caspian Sea and the Black Sea; in 1398 he invaded most of India and sacked Delhi; he then turned west again and invaded Syria and Asia Minor. He died in 1405 while campaigning in China.

In an irony of history even during the turbulent period after the Arab invasion and through the rule of the Mongols and Teimurids, indigenous Iranian art, literature, philosophy, and science flourished.

Shakespeare was apparently aware of early Persian history. In addition to references to Cyrus, Cambyses, Darius, and Tamerlane in his plays he writes of parts of the Persian Empire such as Media and Parthia and lesser-known areas such as the Taurus Mountains and the province of Hyrcania.

THE SAFAVID DYNASTY

Beginning with the Mongol overthrow of the Seljuqs in 1220 through Teimur's conquest of the entire Middle East, Iran was ruled by these conquerors and their descendants. Only a few isolated regions were led by indigenous Iranian tribes. It is with the advent of the Safavid dynasty that Iran was again ruled by ethnic Iranians. The Safavid dynasty overlapped the Tudors and the age of Shakespeare.

The ancestors of the Safavids came from Ardebil, the then principal city in the province of Azerbaijan. Ardebil had been destroyed by the Mongols and never regained its preeminence.[10] The Safavids began as a mystic order circa 1300 named for Shaykh Safi al Din Abul-Fatah Eshaq who lived and died in a retreat in Ardebil. They were of Iranian descent, not Central Asian. They were probably Sunni Moslems as most of

---

10. Tabriz, a smaller city in Azerbaijan, had been spared by paying a large indemnity to the invaders and eventually became the first Safavid capital.

the population was at the time, but gradually it became a Shi'a movement.[11]

By the end of his life Safi al Din had gathered a large following. After his death, his sons, grandsons, and great-grandsons spread the Shi'a doctrine further, and by the beginning of the fifteenth century Shi'ism had reached most Iranian provinces and cities. Haydar, the great grandson of Safi al Din, had become the de facto ruler of most provinces. He acted as the highest authority in temporal and religious matters.

The then ruling dynasty the Aq Quyunlus were unable to deal with the insurrections that had arisen in various parts of the country. Haydar and his son Ali were killed in battle against the Aq Quyunlus. Ali's son Isma'il, who was no more than fourteen and had been protected by the local rulers of Gilan province, became the legitimate head of the order. The Safavids had prepared a genealogy showing that they were descended from the Seventh Shi'ite Imam, Mousa al Kazem, which had been readily accepted by the faithful. In a crucial battle in 1502 near the present-day city of Baku, Isma'il's forces defeated the main army

---

11. Safi al Din claimed descent from the Twelfth Imam who is believed by Shi'ites to have gone into occultation in A.D. 874 and would return on the Day of Judgment.

of the Aq Quyunlus with vital support from a confederation of Shi'ite tribes named Qezelbash.[12]

Isma'il was crowned king in 1502. In one of his first acts he proclaimed Shi'ism the official creed of his realm. The measure gave the dynasty a strong ideological basis and further united the country against its Sunni neighbors.[13] The Shi'ite state that Isma'il created was surrounded by Sunni countries and there were still Sunni majorities in a few provinces of Iran. The situation continued to be perilous, but when in 1510 Isma'il's forces defeated the Sunni Uzbeks who had overrun and occupied the eastern province of Khorasan, the nascent state and the Safavid throne were secure.

----

12. The Qezelbash were a Turkish-speaking tribe of Iranian origin who were fervent Shi'ites. Isma'il rewarded them with some of the lands they had conquered. With the coming of Shah Tahmasb their fervor subsided. After Tahmasb they became merely an unruly band wanting to be kingmakers. They killed the crown prince and several other princes and functionaries. Shah Abbas on assuming the throne took measures to check their power.

13. The schism among Moslems took place shortly after the Prophet's death in A.D. 622 over the issue of succession. Sunnis believe the rightful heirs were Abu Bakr, Omar, and Osman who had been notable followers of the prophet. Shi'as believe that the rightful successor was Ali, the cousin and son-in-law of the Prophet, and thereafter the children of Ali and Fatemeh Zahra, the Prophet's daughter. The Shi'as argued that succession could not be relegated to those not related by blood to the Prophet. The issue became further poisoned when in the struggle Ali was assassinated.

It was clear from the outset, however, that the Ottoman Turks,[14] as defenders of Sunni Islam, would feel
threatened by having a Shi'ite state on their eastern
border. It was only a matter of time before the Turks
would move on Iran. Pro-Safavid/Shi'ite inspired revolts in the eastern Ottoman provinces gave Sultan Selim (The Grim) the pretense on which to launch a full-
scale invasion of Iran. The real purpose was to do away

---

14. The Ottomans were the last of the major tribes of
Turkish origin to invade the Near East. They settled in
what is now modern Turkey. After the breakdown of the
Turkish Seljuq dynasty that ruled Iran they occupied most
of Asia Minor and parts of Central Asia and began to
emerge as the great regional power. Their name derives
from Osman I (1259–1326) who had begun his career in
the service of the Seljuq Turks. In 1299 he established
a kingdom of his own and assumed the title of sultan.
He conquered a great part of Asia Minor, founding the
Ottoman Empire. Its subsequent conquests were parts
of the Byzantine Empire, which included Serbia, then
Kosovo in 1365, and what is now Hungary. In 1453 they
captured Constantinople, which was the end of the
Byzantine Empire and the emergence of the Ottomans
as a major power in Eastern Europe. They also extended
their rule to parts of western Iran, the Arabian Peninsula,
Syria, and Egypt. Their success was greatly due to their
superior military organization. Their deepest penetration
in Europe was in 1683 when they laid siege to Vienna but
were forced to withdraw. Thereafter there was a steady
decline and a succession of weak rulers (as in Iran).
Their rulers spent most of their time in the harem and in
excessive consumption of alcohol. The Ottoman Empire
lasted until its breakup after the end of World War I. The
revival of Turkey as a great nation is in large part due to
the emergence in the twentieth century of a leader of the
caliber of Mostafa Kamal Ataturk.

with Shah Isma'il and end the nascent Safavid dynasty. It began in 1509 with a massacre of Shi'ites in Ottoman dominions. Shortly thereafter there was a major invasion that culminated in the battle of Chaldiran, a small town near the modern city of Khoy in northwest Iran. It was a one-sided battle as the Ottoman forces were equipped with canons and handguns while the Iranians for reasons not entirely clear chose not to use the limited firearms and canons they had. Iranians answered with swords and suffered a humiliating defeat. Isma'il and his commanders appear to have relied on Shi'ite fervor, believing their faith would prevail over the superior arms of the Ottomans. Shortly thereafter there was a siege of Tabriz, but Selim's army, having traveled some five hundred kilometers carrying canons over hills and mountains, mutinied, and the Ottomans chose to withdraw.

Isma'il died in 1524 at age thirty-seven and was buried in Ardebil. Most commentators believe he must have been a charismatic leader who attracted a large following and established a dynasty that would rule for over two hundred years. It is equally held that he lacked technical brilliance in battle. The overwhelming defeat at Chaldiran broke his spirit and he never thereafter led his men in battle.

Tahmasp (1524–76), the eldest son of Isma'il, succeeded to the throne at age ten. Once again the Qezelbash played a key part in ensuring a smooth transition. They selected a regent who was to be the de

CONCORDIA COLLEGE LIBRARY
BRONXVILLE, NY 10708

facto ruler until Tahmasp came of age. It would take nearly ten years until Tahmasp extended his authority over the Qezelbash and other unruly tribal forces and gained control over the eastern provinces. The need to fight on two fronts, the Uzbeks, a Sunni Turkic people, in the east and the Ottomans in the west, weakened the state. The Ottomans mounted several major campaigns between 1533 and 1534. In 1534 Baghdad and its surrounding area fell to the Ottomans and shortly thereafter Tabriz was occupied. Both campaigns were indecisive and the Ottomans withdrew their forces. Tahmasp launched several campaigns in the Caucasus between 1540 and 1553. Large numbers of Georgian, Circassian, and Armenian prisoners were settled in Iran. They enriched the state by their diversity and by the time of Shah Abbas I, Armenians had a near monopoly of the lucrative silk trade. In 1555 a treaty was signed between Iran and the Ottomans that recognized Ottoman sovereignty over Iraq and eastern Anatolia while leaving Iran in control of Azerbaijan and the eastern Caucasus. Somehow the country held together. In 1561, however, Tahmasp was forced to move the capital from Tabriz to Qazvin, a city farther from Ottoman lands.

By the time Tahmasp died in 1576 the Safavids had demonstrated their viability despite an inferior military organization, an unruly Qezelbash, and a weakening in ideology and Shi'a fervor. On Tahmasp's death the throne passed to his son Isma'il II, whose brief and bloody reign lasted a mere two years. Isma'il II was poisoned in 1577. The only member of the Safavid dynasty who had been spared was Isma'il's son Mohammad Khodabandeh, a pious ascetic who became the next ruler.

The military position of the state worsened during this period of uncertainty. There was a resurgence of Qezelbash interference and much fighting in their ranks. The Uzbeks from the east mounted several attacks on Khorasan province in 1578. The Ottomans despite their treaty obligations occupied Tabriz in 1585 and remained in occupation for nearly twenty years. Between 1587 and 1590 the Ottomans mounted several campaigns and occupied Ganje in Azerbaijan and the provinces of Lurestan and Khuzestan.

SHAH ABBAS I

When Shah Abbas (1587–1629), a grandson of Shah Tahmasp, ascended the throne in 1587 Iran was in a dire situation. In the east the Uzbeks had occupied Balkh and Herat, and Khorasan had been once again overrun. In the west all Iranian provinces along the border with Ottoman territory, including the former capital Tabriz, were under Ottoman occupation. The central government was weak and short of funds. There was civil unrest and the Qezelbash who had been instrumental in Abbas coming to the throne pressed for a greater role in the administration of the government and the appointment of individuals to key posts.

Abbas had no intention to give them a more prominent role. Slowly he removed Qezelbash officials from
high positions and sent them to distant provinces. He
reorganized the army, changing the key personnel. He
also brought in members of the Shahsavan tribe to balance the influence of the Qezelbash whose affluence
had weakened their religious fervor.

In recovering lost territories Shah Abbas bided his
time. The Uzbeks had launched several invasions
and had occupied Balkh, Herat, Mashhad, and Nayshabur in the province of Khorasan. By the end of
1597 they had been driven from Khorasan. In a battle
near Herat the leader of the Uzbeks was killed and the
area was pacified. Abbas then turned his attention to
the Ottomans. He launched a well-planned campaign
to dislodge them from Baghdad, which fell after an
eight-month siege. The fall of Baghdad weakened the
morale of the Turks and their garrisons at Mosul and
Kirkuk fell in quick succession. With his victory in
Baghdad, Shah Abbas made a pilgrimage to the revered Shi'ite centers of Karbela, Najaf, Kazemain, and
Samara. Then in 1603 Abbas recaptured Tabriz, Ye-
revan, Shirvan, and Kars, and the following year defeated the Turks near Lake Urumieh and recovered all
of Azerbaijan and Kurdestan. However, wars with the
Ottomans continued to the end of his rule.

Abbas maintained a distance from the clergy. He
devised greater separation of religious and secu-
lar power and exercised control over the theocratic

state. The influence of the leading theologians over affairs of state was reduced. Abbas argued that as a descendant of the last Imam he was the final authority in matters of both state and theology. The religious leaders had no alternative but to submit. Abbas even appointed capable Christian Armenians to administrative positions. Armenians had been moved from Shirvan around 1578 and later by Soltan Mohammad Khodabandeh. Large numbers were relocated in 1604 to Isfahan and its environs. They developed the silk industry. They thrived and became wealthy. Efforts by the Iranian clergy to convert them to Islam failed. Shah Abbas allowed them to establish two Christian schools in Isfahan, St. Pierre, and St. Paul. Armenians were also instrumental in establishing relations with the Vatican.

Abbas was open-minded and by temperament a moderate although he could also be ruthless. Though the wars with the Ottomans continued until the end of his rule he found time to devote to several favorite projects. The city of Isfahan was essentially his creation and he made it his capital in 1600–1601. The core of the city was Naqsh-e Jahan, a magnificent square some seven times the size of the Piazza San Marco in Venice. Around the square were the Ali Qapu Palace with extraordinary interior architectural features; the royal bazaar with its vaulted ceilings housing master artisans working with base and precious metals, fabrics, and carpets; two of the greatest mosques in the world,

Masjed Shah and later Masjed Sheikh Lotfallah. Under Abbas, Isfahan became a prosperous city. Merchants from China, India, Central Asia, and Europe traveled there to buy goods produced by Iranian artisans.

Abbas also developed Mashhad, the capital of Khorasan, which houses the tomb of Imam Reza, the eighth Imam, as a major center of Shi'a pilgrimage. His initiative brought to the Iranian treasury large sums of money that otherwise would have been spent at the principal Shi'ite shrines in Mesopotamia (modern-day Iraq), which was mostly in Ottoman hands. He also developed the northern province of Mazandaran on the Caspian Sea and built a palace at Ashraf (Behshahr of today) where he spent his summers.

Iran in the sixteenth century was isolated. There were no relations with the inhabitants of the neighboring lands who were predominantly Sunni. Equally important was that Iran was shut off from access to the Persian Gulf by the Portuguese domination of the vital southern islands of Bahrain and Hormuz since the early 1500s. The Portuguese had blocked the Persian Gulf not only to Iran but to any trading partners to the east and west.

Abbas was the first Safavid ruler to establish control over the Persian Gulf, an area long held by Arab tribes. He realized that the Portuguese domination of Hormuz must end and the entire area be freed of Portuguese occupation. He finally managed to drive the Portuguese from Hormuz with the assistance of the

English navy in 1622. The English themselves were seeking trade advantages in the region.

Shah Abbas was the greatest of the Safavid rulers. Foremost he was a just monarch. He was also an outstanding strategist, which compensated for the weak military forces he had inherited. He recaptured all the territories that had been lost by his predecessors. He never received any military help despite assurances from princes of Europe and the Vatican for a joint front against the Ottomans. He encouraged trade and commerce with the West. He was the driving force behind the Armenians' expansion of the silk trade that enriched the state treasury.

A fitting epitaph for Shah Abbas was written some thirty-five years after his death by the Frenchman Jean Chardin, a seventeenth century frequent traveler to Iran with a reputation as an astute observer: "When the Great Prince ceased to live, Persia ceased to prosper." Abbas's fame soon spread to London. The references to the Sophy in Shakespeare's plays stem from the fame and renown of Shah Abbas in the West.[15]

THE DECLINE OF THE SAFAVIDS

Shah Abbas had no direct male successor when he died in 1629. His grandson Safi, who had spent his youth in the confines of the harem, became the ruler. Travelers relate stories of his cruelty. Safi died in 1642

---

15. See *The Merchant of Venice* and *Twelfth Night* (pages 103 and 111).

at age thirty, probably from excessive consumption of alcohol.

On Safi's death the throne went to Abbas II (1642–67). The decline continued. On Shah Abbas II's death Shah Soleyman came to the throne (1667–94). He was totally incompetent. Beginning with the reign of Soleyman there was a growing influence of the religious establishment that had progressively freed itself from all administrative control. Powerful theologians such as Mohammad Baqer Majlesi had gained prominence and a large following. Soleyman seemed oblivious to the growing power and influence of the clergy in matters of state. By the end of his reign all decisions had to have the approval of the clergy.[16]

Next to rule was Soleyman's son Shah Soltan Hoseyn (1694–1722), the weakest and most incompetent ruler of the Safavid dynasty. He too was surrounded by members of the clergy who influenced and even directed his every move. There were insurrections in almost all parts of the country. Security on the roads and in the towns that travelers had praised in their

---

16. The rise of the influence of the clergy forced the young to concentrate on theological studies at the expense of science and mathematics. It also limited the possibilities of theater to passion plays. This was the era when Europe was making great advances in every area of scientific endeavor and thought. The age of Galileo, Kepler, Newton, and the philosophers Spinoza and Descartes. The clergy also eliminated the possibility of the development of the theater beyond passion plays for holy days.

writings disappeared. Caravans of goods were robbed even at Isfahan's gates.

Some ten years later (1709) there was an attack by Afghan tribal chieftain Mir Vays who had established the Ghilzai dynasty in Qandahar, which had been ruled by Safavids since Abbas I. Mir Vays defeated the Iranian forces in a short time. He died in 1715 and his son Mahmoud and later Mahmoud's cousin Ashraf proclaimed themselves shah. Ashraf's territory was small. The Afghans were not the only neighbors to sense the decay and imminent collapse of the Safavid Empire. Soon the Ottomans invaded western Iran. The Afghans saw their chance and broke into Isfahan after a long siege and massacred all princes of royal blood and then indiscriminately killed residents of the city.

Some historians have argued that the Safavid state as built by Shah Isma'il, Tahmasp, and Abbas I had an imposing façade that concealed its hollowness and later decay. However, the Safavids brought stability and progress, and more important they held the country together.

Even a brief review of the Safavid era would not be complete without reference to Jean Chardin's memorable account of his travels to and residence in Persia in the seventeenth century. Jean Chardin (1643–1713) was a jeweler merchant not associated with any trading company. His first journey to the East was in 1664 and he reached Persia in 1665 during the reign of Shah

Abbas II who made him his official jeweler. He stayed in Isfahan for over a year. He moved east to India and on his return stopped in Persia in 1669.

His second and most notable journey was between 1671 and 1673 during Shah Soleyman's reign, about which he later wrote. [17] On 1 November 1666 he reports Persia is in irreversible decline. In general he bemoans the great power of Persian kings whom he observes have greater authority than those in Europe and comments on their indolence and indifference to the welfare of the people. From what he had heard he considers Shah Abbas I as a visionary.

Chardin gives descriptions of other major Iranian cities but is most taken by the architecture and beauty of Isfahan. He gives detailed accounts of his beloved city of Isfahan and offers astute observations on everyday life. He blends this with social commentary and anecdotes.

He comments on the hygiene, health standards, and the availability of public baths. He states Isfahan is as large and populous as London. He explains that Isfahan has a circumference of some twenty-four miles, twelve gates, 162 mosques, forty-eight madrassas, 1802 caravanserai, 273 public baths, twelve cemeteries, and a population of more than a million. He praises the fresh air of Isfahan and adds that it is unneces-

---

17. Jean Chardin, *The Travels of John Chardin into Persia and the East Indies* (London, 1691).

sary to cork a bottle of wine; you merely need to insert a rose or carnation in the mouth of the bottle.

During the Safavid period epic narrations of the lives, wars, and great deeds of the kings recited in coffeehouses by itinerant storytellers became popular. As were dramatic recitations of the great store of Persian poetry. Chardin believed that poetry was a natural medium of expression for Persians because of the softness of the language.[18]

The great contributions of the Safavids to the arts are in architecture and painting. Poetry, which through the ages had been the distinguishing feature of Iranian culture, fails badly during their reign. Notable scholars of Iranian literature – Edward G. Browne, Mohammad Qazvini, and Dr. Ghasem Ghani – are on record that not a single poet of the first rank can be named in the two-hundred-year span of the Safavid era.

The Safavids were the artistic heirs of the brilliant school of painting developed at the Teimurid court at Herat and Khorasan. When Shah Isma'il selected

---

18. Chardin relates a story that captures the very tone and essence of three languages: Arabic, Persian, and Turkish. According to the story the serpent in the Garden of Eden spoke in Arabic because it was the language of logic and persuasion; Adam and Eve spoke in Persian because it was soft and insinuating; when the angel Gabriel wanted to order Adam and Eve out of the Garden of Eden, he first spoke in Arabic, then Persian, neither of which had the desired effect. He therefore used Turkish, a language of harsh consonants, and Adam and Eve obeyed.

Tabriz as his capital, he made Herat the second city of his fledgling empire. Isma'il took a group of artists from Herat and established the Tabriz school of painting. The famous copy of the *Shahnameh* (The Book of Kings) of the poet Ferdowsi produced under the patronage of Shah Tahmasp, before its separation and dispersal among collectors and museums, contained more than 250 paintings. During Shah Abbas I's reign there was the great painter Reza Abbasi. The art of calligraphy reached perfection under Mir Emad, Soltan Ali Mashhadi, and Mir Ali Heravi.

The Safavid dynasty ended ingloriously but left an important legacy.

TRAVELERS TO PERSIA AND
COMMERCIAL RELATIONS

There had been contact between Iran and the West from the earliest history of the Persian Empire. Even the wars of the Achaemenians with Greece, and the Parthians and Sasanians with Rome, established contacts that later led to commercial and cultural exchanges. In pre-Islamic Parthian times the cult of Mitra the Persian God of Light was brought to Rome and further west, and for a brief period it rivaled Christianity in numbers of adherents. Later Manichaeism, the dualist cult founded by the Persian Mani, which embraced some elements of Christianity, spread as far west as France.[1] There was also a West to East flow. As early as the ninth to eleventh centuries there were Christian converts in several Persian cities. Some elements of religious diversity are evidenced in Nayshabur pottery and artifacts of the time.[2]

One of the earliest accounts of travel to Iran by a Westerner is by the Venetian Marco Polo (circa 1254 to circa 1324) during Iran's occupation by Mongol conquerors. Together with his father and uncle, Nicolo and Maffeo Polo, he traveled overland to China in 1271 to the court of Kublai Khan, the ruler of China. Both on the outward journey and the return to Venice the party stayed for some time in Iran. There was a second journey some seventeen years later to China and back through Iran. There is still some controversy as to the exact route Marco Polo took in Iran, but it is known he visited Tabriz, Kashan, and Kerman. Marco Polo and his party were purely merchants and there is little

---

1. Though suppressed in Iran as a heresy its success in the West was such that St. Augustine in his youth had become a temporary convert to Manichaeism in the seventh century.

2. Charles K. Wilkinson, "Remains from Nayshabur," *Forschungen zur Kunst Asiens*, (Istanbul, 1970). Wilkinson, a leading authority on Nayshabur pottery, convincingly argues that there was a Christian community in Nayshabur in the mid-ninth through eleventh centuries, as symbols of various religions including Christianity appear on the acclaimed Nayshabur pottery of the period.

of historical value in their written accounts.[3] During the Renaissance it was the primary Western source of information on most parts of Central Asia and it was important as the first account of Iran since the Arab invasion. Iran once again became a reality to Europeans after an absence of more than six hundred years.

There were contacts with Europeans during the Teimurid period and there are even records of Teimur having written letters in Persian to Charles VI of France desiring to continue their correspondence to protect merchants traveling between East and West.[4] There are two later travelers of note who have left records of their journey to Persia. Ruy Gonzales De Clavijo was a Spanish knight who headed a delegation from Henry III of Castille to the court of Teimur in 1403–4, traveling from Tabriz to Rey, Mashhad, and Samarqand. In Mashhad he visited the shrine of Imam Reza, the eighth Shi'a Imam, and entered the tomb itself to pay his respect. He continued his journey and was well received by people who kissed the hem of his robes for having made the pilgrimage to the shrine. His book demonstrates the Shi'a fervor

---

3. Marco Polo and Nicolo De Conti, *The Most Noble and Famous Travels of Marco Polo Together with Nicolo De Conti.* The book was translated into English circa 1579 by John Frompton. It is likely that Shakespeare and his contemporary playwrights read the English translation.

4. Sylvester de Sacy, *Memoirs de la Institute Royal France* (Paris, 1866), 470–528; quoted by Hassan Javadi, *Persian Literary Influence on English Literature* (Calcutta, 1983), 11.

in Iran even before the advent of the Safavids.[5] The other notable traveler, Josafa Barbaro, was the ambassador of Venice to the court of Uzun Hassan of the "White Sheep dynasty" at Tabriz, which ruled part of the northwest provinces of Persia. His stay was from 1467 to 1478. Barbaro also traveled to central Iran, including the city of Yazd.[6]

VENICE AND PORTUGAL

Prior to the beginning of the sixteenth century Venice had been the supreme trading power in the Near and Far East, but events in the fifteenth century dealt a great blow to Venetian supremacy. The first was the capture of Constantinople by the Ottomans in 1453. The second was the discovery by the Portuguese in 1487 of the sea route around the Cape of Good Hope to the Middle East and the East Indies.

The Portuguese came to the East not merely as traders but as conquerors. The Portuguese general Alfonso de Albuquerque correctly identified the three key points that would dominate all trade between East and West as the Gulf of Aden (linking the

---

5. *Narrative of the Embassy of Ruy Gonzales De Clavijo to the Court of Timour at Samarqand 1403–1406,* translated from the original Spanish into English in 1859 (London, 1971).

6. Josafa Barbaro and Ambrogio Contarini, *Travels to Tana and Persia* (London, 1873).

Indian Ocean to the Red Sea), the Strait of Hormuz (linking the Gulf of Oman to the Persian Gulf), and the Strait of Malacca (linking the Indian Ocean to the South China Sea). He captured the island of Hormuz from the Arabs in 1509 and returned in 1515 to secure the Portuguese hold. With the subsequent occupation of the nearby island of Qeshm, Portugal controlled the entrance to the Persian Gulf. The establishment of the Portuguese in the Persian Gulf and the Indian Ocean changed the pattern of trade. The Persian Gulf had been one of the main routes of East-West trade through which the products of China, the Malay Archipelago, India, and Persia were sent to Europe.

Traditionally the basis of Venetian prosperity was in transactions involving oriental merchandise. The ancient route from the East ran through the Persian Gulf, the Euphrates Valley, and across the desert (or alternately by the Red Sea and Isthmus of Suez) to the Mediterranean where silk, precious stones, spices, and medicinal drugs were purchased by the Venetians and sold throughout Europe. Now with the Portuguese strong fortress on Hormuz near the mouth of the Persian Gulf they could shut off that route. The grand design of the Portuguese was to force all trade between Europe and the East to go around the Cape of Good Hope. All cargoes being allowed to pass through the Strait of Hormuz were to be carried by Portuguese vessels for a fee and a surcharge laid on the vessels.

The Venetians, contemplating their dwindling revenues, were hopeful that the English would drive the Portuguese from Eastern commerce and particularly from their base in the Persian Gulf at Hormuz.

ENGLAND'S COMMERCE WITH PERSIA

As late as the first decade of the sixteenth century England was considered backward in commerce, lagging behind Spain, Portugal, and the republic of Venice. The Portuguese under Alfonso de Albuquerque, viceroy of Portuguese Indies, acquired Goa, Ceylon, Malacca, and Hormuz. The Spaniard Hernando Cortez was conquering Mexico and fellow Spaniards were gaining control of the Philippine Islands. The changes in England came thereafter. By the middle of the sixteenth century the English began to be more aggressive. England had good scientists, geographers, mathematicians, and navigators such as John Cabot and his son Sebastian Cabot and the geographer Richard Hakluyt.[7] With the end of the war with Spain in 1588 public interest in exploration became an avid Protestant activity – to spread the new faith by planting English stock on the coast of North America.[8]

---

7. A.L. Rowse, *The Expansion of Elizabethan England* (University of Wisconsin, 1955).

8. Ibid.

In early 1553 The Mysterie and Company of Merchant Adventurers for the Discovery of Regions, Dominions, Islands and Places Unknown had been formed in London with Sebastian Cabot as its first governor. One of the initial objects of the company was to bypass Ottoman-held territory and the Portuguese-dominated Persian Gulf. Toward that end the new company attempted to find a northwest passage to China. After discovery of the northern Russian port of Archangel the company was successively renamed "The Muscovy Company" and "The Russia Company." It was the first joint stock company formed for foreign trade. Two of the ships that had set out in 1553 were lost in stormy weather north of Norway, but the third under the command of Richard Chancellor reached Archangel. Then they traveled by land to Moscow and obtained traveling privileges from Ivan IV (The Terrible), tsar of Russia. However, on his return through Archangel, Chancellor lost his life.[9]

Despite the losses another English merchant and experienced seaman Anthony Jenkinson (d. 1611) and two brothers Richard and Robert Johnson made another attempt and reached Archangel safely. They too traveled south by land and were received by Ivan the Terrible. Jenkinson in his youth had been employed by the Levant Company trading with the eastern lands of the Mediterranean. He had then been called to take

---

9. Shakespeare has several references to Muscovites and Russian travel in *Love's Labour's Lost*. (See page 99.)

charge of the Russian market. Jenkinson won the confidence of the tsar, who gave him backing for his journey to Persia and entrusted him to trade on his behalf as well as that of The Muscovy Company. The plan was to sail across the Caspian Sea and land either in Gilan or Mazandaran, provinces of northern Persia. Jenkinson traveled to Astrakhan and crossed the Caspian; however, he landed on the eastern shores of the Caspian in Central Asia, in non-Persian territory. It was nonetheless a pioneering effort and he had discovered a route to Central Asia bypassing Ottoman-held territory.

In 1562 Jenkinson took two ships to cross the Caspian, this time landing on its western shores in Safavid territory. He was received by the governor, Abdallah Khan Ustajlu, Shah Tahmasp's brother-in-law and cousin. He then traveled south and on 20 November 1562 arrived in Qazvin, then the capital. Jenkinson was probably the first Englishman to visit Persia. He was received in audience by Shah Tahmasp and he handed him letters from the tsar and Queen Elizabeth. All went well until the shah was told that Jenkinson was a Christian and further negotiations ceased. But all was not lost as Abdallah Khan interceded with Shah Tahmasp who relented and gave Jenkinson a handsome gift when he left. Later Abdallah Khan himself granted trading privileges to The Muscovy Company.[10] On Jenkinson's third trip he obtained important

10. Roger Savory, *Iran Under the Safavids* (Cambridge University Press, 1980), 112.

concessions: the full monopoly of all trade in and out of Persia by the northern route and license to trade in Russian territory. In 1571, however, the accord was broken and there were mutual recriminations. The tsar had wanted an English bride from amongst the ladies in waiting to Queen Elizabeth. The queen dismissed the request and the tsar annulled all privileges. Somehow Jenkinson regained favor and returned one last time in 1571–72.

A few years after Jenkinson's visit to the court of Shah Tahmasp, Ivan the Terrible was considering a joint military action with Tahmasp against the Ottomans. In 1569 he sent an envoy, Dolmet Karpivicz, with gifts of canons of various sizes and some muskets. The tsar offered to send musketeers to instruct and drill Persians in their use. Shah Tahmasp was happy with the gifts and offered to aid the tsar "to the best of his ability."[11] There is no record of whether the proposal got any further.

It soon became apparent that the Archangel route was too dangerous and it was abandoned. The overland route from Aleppo to the Persian Gulf had met with no more success as merchants had to travel through the Ottoman-held lands of Syria and Mesopotamia. It was clear that the Portuguese hold on the Persian Gulf had to be broken if English commerce was to thrive. In 1602 Shah Abbas had driven the Portuguese from Bahrain, but he was realistic and knew

---

11. Ibid.

he could not hope to expel them from their fortress at Hormuz without superior naval power. The basis for cooperation with England was slowly beginning to take shape.

In 1600 Queen Elizabeth had chartered a commercial company named the East India Company, which was given a monopoly of trade between East and West. In 1615 the East India Company made its first attempt to break into the Iranian market. An officer of the company had realized that northern Persian winters could be very cold and that there would be a good market for English broadcloth. Shortly thereafter the company sent two of its employees to Isfahan and soon a market was established. Shah Abbas issued a *farman* (royal decree) giving the East India Company the right to trade throughout the country.[12] England was to send an ambassador to Persia. English nationals were granted the right to practice their religion and in legal matters to be under the jurisdiction of their ambassador.[13]

12. By the end of the eighteenth century the East India Company had become in effect the ruler of a large part of India that was governed by the company's officers and a committee responsible to Parliament. The company was dissolved in 1858.

13. The granting of extraterritorial rights to England and later other countries had a devastating effect on Iran, and by the end of the nineteenth century virtually all European nationals were under the sole jurisdiction of their embassies. Extraterritorial rights were not abolished until early in the twentieth century during the reign of Reza Shah.

Domestic trade, which had been mostly in the hands of Persian Moslem and Jewish merchants, remained intact despite the inroads of the East India Company. Foreign trade had been almost exclusively the domain of Persian Armenians. The largest source of revenue in the royal treasury was the silk trade. With improved relations with England, Shah Abbas designated the East India Company to handle the export of silk. In 1615 Shah Abbas issued another farman authorizing the East India Company to establish plants at Jask, Shiraz, and Isfahan. The stage was set for a joint Anglo-Persian attempt to mount an attack on Hormuz and drive the Portuguese out. In 1622 the joint effort ended Portugal's domination of the Persian Gulf. A Portuguese attempt to recapture Hormuz in 1625 failed. Soon thereafter Charles II dispatched the first English ambassador, Sir Dodmore Cotton, a member of King Charles's Privy Chamber, to the court of Shah Abbas. Sir Dodmore was accompanied by Sir Robert Sherley who had lived in Persia from 1598 but had been away in Europe since 1615.[14] The party reached Shah Abbas's palace at Farahabad in 1627. Sir Dodmore died shortly after his audience and presentation of his credentials in Isfahan.

---

14. Another Englishman who accompanied Sir Dodmore was Thomas Herbert who later wrote an entertaining book on his impressions of Persia, *A Relation of Some Years Traveile Begunne Anno 1626 into Afrique and the Greater Part of Asia, Especially the Territories of the Persian Monarchie* (London, 1634).

Robert Sherley and his brother Anthony had set out in 1598 on a journey to Persia financed by the Earl of Essex to enlist Persian military help against the Ottoman Turks, the common foe, who were making conquests in both Europe and Persia. A further purpose was to assess commercial possibilities. Their stay in Persia and their extensive travels abroad on behalf of Shah Abbas became widely known and exaggerated in England. Their story is told in detail in the following chapter.

SHAKESPEARE AND SOUTHAMPTON; ESSEX AND THE SHERLEYS' PERSIAN VENTURE

More has been written of Anthony and Robert Sherley's travels to Persia in Shakespeare's time during the reign of Shah Abbas I than any other travelers of that era. Contact with Persia was not then a new thing, but the Sherley ventures attracted an inordinate amount of attention. In their lifetime three books were written giving a glowing account of their arduous journey.[1] Even Anthony Sherley himself

---

1. William Parry, "A New and Large Discourse of the Travels of Sir Anthonie Sherley, Knight by Sea and Overland to the Persian Empire" (London, 1601).
An anonymous pamphlet was compiled by Anthony Nixon in 1607 and registered in 1615. (It was republished in 1825 under the pen of George Manwaring who had accompanied Anthony and Robert Sherley.)
An account by Abel Pinçon first published in 1651 in Paris with the title: *"Relation d'un voyages faités és années 1598 et 1599 par un gentilhomme de la suitte du Seigneur Scierley, Ambassadeur du Roy d'Angleterre."*
Several pamphlets were published between 1600 and 1603 that were suppressed by authorities. The sole remaining copy is kept at the British Museum. The probable reason for the suppression was that the voyage of the Sherleys had been sponsored by the Earl of Essex who was then in disgrace and later executed for treason.

wrote a self-serving account.[2] Books and articles continued to be written in the nineteenth and twentieth centuries.[3]

The adventures of the Sherley brothers even reached the London stage in an absurd dramatization by two lesser-known playwrights based on Anthony Nixon's 1607 pamphlets. The play's end reaches an absurd height with the "Sophy," Shah Abbas I, ordering Robert Sherley to build a church saying, "The Persian children shall be brought up and know no other education, manners, language, or religion, than what by Christians is deliver'd to them."[4]

Robert Sherley and his Circasian wife Teresia were painted by Anthony Van Dyke, the foremost court painter of England. Their portraits are exhibited in Petworth House in Sussex and often at the National Portrait Gallery in London. A portrait in Persian costume

---

2. Sir Anthony's book was published in 1613 under the title, *Sir Anthony Shirley, His Relation of His Travels in Persia. The Dangers and Distress Which Befell Him.*

3. The nineteenth- and twentieth-century books include: George Manwaring, *The Three Brothers* (London, 1825); S. W. Chew, *The Crescent and the Rose* (Oxford, 1937); D. W. Davies, *Elizabethans Errant: The Strange Fortune of Sir Thomas Sherley and His Three Sons* (United States, 1967); and several authoritative articles in various journals, listed in the bibliography.

4. John Day, William Rowley and George Williams, *The Travails of Three English Brothers, Sir Thomas, Sir Anthony, Mr. Robert Sherley*, first acted at the Red Bull Theatre in 1607. From Dr. Hassan Javadi, "Persian Literary Influence on English Literature" (Calcutta, 1983): 20.

has hung in the National Portrait Gallery. There is a reference to Persian opulent attire in *King Lear*.[5]

Various English and Persian writers credit Anthony with introducing canonry and muskets into Persia and Robert Sherley, age seventeen or eighteen with limited experience in warfare, with reorganizing the Iranian army, enabling it to withstand the might of the Ottoman Empire. In making an assessment of Anthony Sherley's exaggerated reputation among the English, the following point may not be irrelevant: In 1888 the Reverend Scott Surtee, of Dinsdale-on-Tees, published a pamphlet entitled, "William Shakespeare of Stratford-on-Avon," in which he assigned to Sir Anthony Sherley the honor of having written Shakespeare's plays.[6] Recent scholarship has acquainted us with a more balanced and accurate picture of the brothers' lives.

The euphoria created by the defeat of the Spanish Armada encouraged a public demand for heroic deeds by Englishmen. It is plain that the Sherleys had captured the imagination of the English public. It was inevitable that their story would become the subject of at least one play, poems, and travel books. In any

---

5. *King Lear,* III, 6, 78–81 (See page 142).

6. Savory, "The Sherley Myth": 81. Quoting from "Dictionary of National Biography" (Loc Cit): 124.

event, Persia and the Safavid monarchy entered into English literature.[7]

There were a number of other factors which would have drawn Shakespeare's attention toward the Sherleys and their travel to distant Persia. Shakespeare even may have been privy to the origin of Sherley's voyage as it involved the Earl of Essex who was closely associated with the Earl of Southampton, Shakespeare's benefactor.

It is nearly certain that Shakespeare had met Southampton earlier through the playhouse. Southampton, like Essex his idol, was a devoted theatergoer. Some commentators, being aware of the vastly different backgrounds of the earl and Shakespeare, have doubts that those of such differing social strata in sixteenth-century England could have associated socially. There could have been intermediaries, however, who facilitated introductions. Peter Ackroyd, a biographer of Shakespeare,[8] argues that some time after the pub-

---

7. Only some twenty years after Shakespeare's death John Milton wrote of the Persian struggle against the Ottomans in *Paradise Lost*:
As when the Tartar from his Russian foe,
By Astracan over the snowy plains
Retires, or Bactrian Sophi, from the horns
Of Turkish crescent, leaves all waste beyond
The realm of Aladule, in his retreat
To Tauris [Tabriz] or Casbeen [Qazvin].
Book X, lines 431–36

8. Peter Ackroyd, *Shakespeare: A Biography* (New York, 2005), 208.

lication of *Venus and Adonis* Southampton's mother, the Countess of Southampton, married Sir Thomas Heneage, who as treasurer of the queen's chamber was responsible for arranging compensation for players who performed at court. He could have introduced Shakespeare to Southampton. Ackroyd further argues that the poet and the earl could have met through Lord Strange who was a good friend of Southampton. Lord Strange's younger brother was an amateur playwright. What could be more natural than that the young earl should be introduced to the most promising play-wright of the day. Furthermore, Lord Strange and the Earl of Southampton were also part of a group of Catholic sympathizers and Southampton was thought by some to be the great hope of the Catholics. Shake-speare because of his parentage fit well with such a group. Southampton was also by a complicated set of circumstances related by marriage to Shakespeare's mother's family, the Ardens of Stratford.

There are several other possible intermediaries, in-cluding Southampton's tutor in French and Italian, John Florio, who was born in London of Protestant refugees from Italy. Ackroyd suggests that Shake-speare may have known Florio and sought his advice on his plays with an Italian setting.[9]

There was also a family connection between South-ampton, Essex, and the Sherleys. While in London Southampton had become enamored of mistress

---

9. Ibid.

Elizabeth Vernon, one of the Queen's ladies in waiting. On his return from a Spanish expedition with Essex his intimacies with mistress Vernon could no longer be concealed as she was seven months pregnant. He had to marry her at the queen's instructions. Elizabeth Vernon's sister Francis married Anthony Sherley. The Vernon sisters were nieces of Essex.

This marriage strengthened the bond between Southampton and Essex and made it inevitable that Southampton would volunteer and indeed insist that he take part in Essex's campaign in Ireland against Tyrone, which ended disastrously for both. Southampton returned with Essex to England with the mission an abject failure. On their return he played an active part in Essex's attempt to remove his enemies and detractors from the court even if it entailed removing the queen from the throne. Both men were tried and condemned to death. Despite the staging of Shakespeare's *Richard II* to incite the crowds on the eve of the planned uprising, Shakespeare's name was not even mentioned at the trial of Essex and Southampton.

Southampton's sentence was commuted to life imprisonment in the Tower of London probably on the recommendation of Sir Robert Cecil, Queen Elizabeth's close advisor, whose father Lord Burleigh had been close to Southampton's father. Southampton was pardoned and given his freedom by James I on his accession to the English throne in 1603.[10] In his last years he was active in the development of the Crown Colony in Virginia. He also served as Lord Lieutenant of the Isle of Wight. He later moved to the House of Lords. Southampton died age fifty-one in 1624.

Southampton is a minor personage in Tudor England. His name acquired some recognition by Shakespeare's dedication of two poems. He rises to prominence through his close association with Essex. As this study indicates Southampton clearly could have been privy to Essex's sponsorship of the Sherleys' travel to Persia.

THE EARL OF ESSEX

Robert Devereux, second Earl of Essex (1566–1601) succeeded to the earldom on the death of his father in 1576 and came under the guardianship of Lord Burleigh. He distinguished himself in the Battle of Zutphen in the Netherlands and was knighted. He returned to England and soon became a favorite of the queen. He had hopes of replacing the aging Lord Burleigh (who died in 1598) as the queen's closest advisor. The queen,

---

10. A. L. Rowse mentions that Shakespeare congratulated Southampton on his liberty in Sonnet cvii. "Shakespeare's Southampton, Patron of Virginia" (London, 1965).
After Southampton's release from the Tower of London, there is no record to indicate he had any contact with Shakespeare.

however, was becoming wary of Essex's ambitions and she gradually conferred the power he sought on Sir Robert Cecil, the son of Lord Burleigh.

Essex became a national figure when he shared command of an expedition that raided Cadiz in 1596. He again became a favorite of the queen. In 1598, he sponsored the voyage of Sir Anthony Sherley and his brother Robert to Persia ostensibly to unite the Christian powers of Europe with Persia to wage wars against the Ottomans who had emerged as the dreaded foe of Europe. An underlying motive was to explore the possibility of lucrative commerce with Persia and neighboring lands.

By this time in early 1598 there was a debate whether to make a permanent peace with Spain. England had been alone in confronting Spain on the continent, in the Netherlands, and on its own shores. There was fear that Spain would aid the rebels in Ireland who were pressing for total independence from England.[11]

Ireland raised a serious threat. The root of the Anglo-Irish relationship can be traced to the twelfth-century Anglo-Norman invasion of Ireland when the English declared themselves lords of Ireland.[12] During the Tudors' reign several key events took place. Henry VIII declared himself king of Ireland and head of the church. By the 1590s the Celtic chiefs opposed

---

11. James Shapiro, *A Year in the Life of William Shakespeare* (Great Britain, 2005), 44–45.

12. Ibid., 51–53.

to English rule united under Ulsterman Hugh O'Neil (known to the English as the Earl of Tyrone). In 1598 Tyrone and his allies inflicted a heavy loss on the English forces at the battle of Black Water.[13] There was even talk of removing the Tudor dynasty.[14] By 1599 London was considering a larger force with a new commander. Essex made himself a candidate. Elizabeth had lost confidence in him, but she finally relented.

Essex left London on 27 March 1599 with a fine army and received a great sendoff by the populace who were certain he would pacify Ireland. Essex's disciple and close friend the Earl of Southampton and others followed him.[15] One of his first acts after landing was to appoint Southampton as General of the Horse in Ireland although Elizabeth had reservations about the appointment.[16] Essex was surprised by the number of rebels he faced who outnumbered his forces by about two to one. From the outset Essex suffered heavy casualties. He asked for parlays with Tyrone knowing full well that the queen had not authorized such talks. He concluded an unauthorized truce and decided to return to London to plead for a larger force. The unpardonable thing was that Essex had discussed with the Irish chieftain

13. Ibid.

14. A. L. Rowse, *The Expansion of Elizabethan England* (University of Wisconsin Press, 2003).

15. Sir Sidney Lee, *A Life of Shakespeare* (London, 1915).

16. Shapiro, *A Year in the Life of William Shakespeare*, 254.

the matter of succession after Elizabeth. It was natural for Elizabeth to become suspicious.[17]

While Essex was on his way to London, Elizabeth had appointed Lord Mountjoy to replace him.[18] Mountjoy was systematic and cautious.[19] He persisted and soon Tyrone's army was decimated. Mountjoy's quick success demonstrated how poorly organized Essex's campaign had been. Most of the Spanish troops fighting with the Irish were also captured or killed.

On his return to London Essex was charged with disobedience to a royal direction and neglect of duty. He was under order to stand trial. Essex, believing that the order had been the work of his enemies at court and that his status with the queen had not altered, attempted to see her. He burst into her dressing room where no man was allowed. Elizabeth was alarmed. She did not know whether Essex was alone or whether

---

17. Essex's reverses were still unknown to the London populace and to Shakespeare. In the prologue to Act V of *Henry V* written at the time, the chorus compares the king's triumphal return from France to that of "the general of our gracious Empress, as in good time he may, from Ireland coming, bringing rebellion broached on his sword." Scholars have long held that the reference is to Essex.

18. Shapiro, *A Year in the Life of William Shakespeare,* 56. Lord Mountjoy's name had been put forward at the initial discussions on appointing the commander of English forces to confront Tyrone.

19. Rowse, *The Expansion of Elizabethan England,* 427.

he might have already killed some of the guards.[20] She ordered Essex arrested and confined to his quarters. It is still unknown whether Essex at the time had any intention of removing the queen.

Essex began to consider removing from the queen's counsels those he considered his personal enemies and to whom he attributed his downfall.[21] Southampton and other men of social position joined in the plot.[22] It has been said that the character of Coriolanus, an intemperate aristocrat, was somehow modeled on Essex.[23]

Essex and his followers decided that the only viable means of eliminating his perceived enemies was the removal of Elizabeth by force if necessary. The best

---

20. Shapiro, *A Year in the Life of William Shakespeare,* 268.

21. Essex's vengefulness against his detractors is further illustrated by the well-known Lopez incident. Dr. Lopez, a Jewish Portuguese physician to Sir Francis Walsingham, Essex, and soon thereafter Queen Elizabeth, was said to be passing around medical information concerning Essex's "shameful anomaly of instincts." On hearing this Essex sought to avenge himself for the insult to his honor. Lopez was accused of being a spy for Spain and also of attempting to poison the queen. He was arrested, tried, and sentenced to death. Elizabeth was reluctant, but popular clamor led to his hanging. Philipa Bernard, "Roderigo Lopez Physician to the Queen," lecture given at Westminster Synagogue, London, 17 February 1987.

22. Shapiro, *A Year in the Life of William Shakespeare,* 272.

23. Frank Kermode, *The Age of Shakespeare* (United States, 2003), 52–57.

way to accomplish it would be by a mass uprising of the people of London and Essex and his band would then storm the palace.[24] Essex and Southampton were both avid theatergoers and special devotees of Shakespeare's plays. Either Essex or Southampton or perhaps even another of the conspirators proposed that a way to arouse the public would be to stage a public performance of Shakespeare's *Richard II*, which depicts Richard's deposition by Henry Bolingbroke, later crowned as Henry IV.[25] The audience would realize that deposition of a monarch had been done before and that there is nothing sacred about a king or queen.

Some conspirators had a meeting with members of Shakespeare's company and persuaded them to

24. Rowse argues that Essex had no alternative as he had discussed with Tyrone the question of succession to the crown.

25. Richard was an incompetent and weak king, but Shakespeare endows him with sublime poetry:
King Richard: What must the King do now? Must he submit?
The King shall do it. Must he be deposed?
The King shall be contented. Must he lose the name of King?
O' God's name let it go.
I'll give my jewels for a set of beads,
My gorgeous palace for a hermitage,
My gay apparel for an almsman's gown,
My figur'd goblet for a dish of wood,
My sceptre for a palmer's walking staff,
My subjects for a pair of carved saints,
And my large kingdom for a little grave,
A little little grave, an obscure grave.
Richard II, Act III, Scene 3, 144–54

perform the play. It is amazing how the theatre and especially the plays of Shakespeare played an important part in the lives of Elizabethans. The mere fact of staging a play to incite the crowds demonstrates its perceived power.

There are various accounts of the events leading to the performance. Frank Kermode[26] suggests that "on the eve of Essex's rebellion, a certain Gelly Mayrick, an officer of Essex's household, commissioned Shakespeare's company to have a special performance of *Richard II*. The actors protested that the play was old, but in the end, for a fee of two pounds, they did as Mayrick requested, including the deposition scene. The play probably had been first performed in 1595 though there is controversy as to whether the scene enacting the actual deposition had been included.[27] Shakespeare must have been torn in two. He was grateful to Southampton, but his intellectual sympathies were with authority and order. In almost all his tragedies order is restored after chaos: Hamlet with Fortinbras; Macbeth with Malcolm; Othello with Cassio; Lear with the Duke of Albany; Antony with Octavius; Julius Caesar with the triumvirate.

On the day after the Globe performance, Essex who had been under house arrest broke out and led his followers into the city where he sought to rally the

26. Kermode, *The Age of Shakespeare,* 51–52.

27. The play was well known and had been in print since 1597 without the deposition scene.

citizenry to his cause, which was probably to arrest the aging queen. The attempt failed disastrously. Essex was arrested for treason on 19 February 1601. The trial was over quickly and he was beheaded on 25 February less than two months after the performance of *Richard II*. As mentioned earlier Southampton was also sentenced to death, but Elizabeth commuted his sentence to life imprisonment in the Tower of London. He was pardoned by King James I after Elizabeth's death. Gelly Mayrick was sentenced to death and hanged. Shakespeare's name was not even mentioned at the trial. By an amazing coincidence on 24 February 1601, the night before the execution of Essex, Shakespeare's company was summoned to perform before the queen.

Harold Bloom best summarizes the reason for the failure of the coup d'état by saying, "Essex was no Bolingbroke and Elizabeth was no Richard II."[28]

Essex's fall was in part responsible for the failure of the Sherley expedition to Persia. It was, however, ill conceived from the beginning. Neither the English government nor the queen had been consulted. In retrospect, it appears that the European powers never had any intention to fight the Turks. It was an attempt to goad Persia to mount a campaign against the Turks and keep them engaged, preventing them from making further incursions in Europe. Furthermore,

28. Harold Bloom, *Shakespeare: The Invention of the Human Mind* (New York, 1999).

Essex's selection of Anthony Sherley to head his venture proved to be a mistake.

THE SHERLEYS

The Sherleys were originally a Warwickshire family that moved to Wiston in Sussex. Their ancestor Hugh Sherley valiantly fought and died for England in 1403. Shakespeare mentions Hugh Sherley in *Henry IV, Part I*:

Prince Henry: Hold up thy head, vile Scot, or thou art like

Never to hold it up again! The spirits

Of valiant Sherley, Stafford, and Blount are in my arms.[29]

Thomas Sherley (or Shirley), a man of means, was born circa 1542. He and his three sons – Thomas, Anthony, and Robert – lived in the England of Elizabeth I and James I. Unlike their ancestor, "They were gentlemen on the make; chicanery, larceny, adultery, heroism, and treachery figured in their story," as related in several books.[30]

---

29. *Henry IV, Part I*, V, 4, 39–43.

30. Most notably D. W. Davies, *Elizabethans Errant: The Strange Fortune of Sir Thomas Sherley and His Three Sons* (United States, 1967), 1–9.

Thomas the elder graduated from Queen's College, Cambridge, in 1561. He returned to Wiston and served as a member of parliament among other positions. He was knighted in 1573. The key event in his early life was when he accompanied an English contingent in 1585 to the Low Countries to assist the Protestant rebels.[31] During the campaign Sir Thomas became the treasurer of the English contingent. In 1597 he suffered a reversal of fortune and was relieved of his duties as treasurer. It was alleged that some funds were unaccounted for. Sir Thomas had also incurred heavy debts and by March 1597 was bankrupt. Sir Thomas the younger also served for a short period in the Low Countries. He too became the treasurer of the contingent and soon thereafter was knighted. After a chequered career as a gentleman adventurer, Thomas settled down and became a member of parliament.

Anthony was not cut in the mould of his older brother. In 1581 at age sixteen he was awarded a Bachelor of Arts degree. He fought in the wars in the Low Countries under the Earl of Leicester. Anthony secretly married Frances Vernon, a first cousin of the Earl of Essex. In 1591, Anthony went to Normandy with Essex in support of Henry of Navarre. Essex

---

31. Spain had occupied the Low Countries. After much debate England in August 1585 sent an army of 6,000 foot and 1,000 horse soldiers under the command of Elizabeth's favorite, Robert Dudley, the Earl of Leicester. The mission was to engage the Spanish, preventing them from strengthening their position.

made a great impression on Anthony, then about twenty-six years of age. Anthony desired to make the earl "the Pattern of his Civil Life, and from him to draw a worthy model of all his actions."[32] While in France, Anthony was made a knight of St. Michael by Henry of Navarre. On his return to England he was imprisoned for his temerity in accepting such an honor without the queen's permission. Elizabeth herself admonished him. Anthony was released on the condition that he surrendered his knighthood. Nevertheless, he continued to allow himself to be commonly called Sir Anthony.[33]

Anthony was restless and it was time to try something new. Sir Francis Drake had returned from one of his voyages with a large hold of Spanish "treasure." Everyone was eager to make a fortune in a short time. Sir Anthony financed by his father had purchased or rented several ships and sailed in May 1596 hoping to raid Spanish vessels and seize their cargo. Nothing worthwhile was gained by these attempts. Anthony was dejected. Also the unhappy marriage to Essex's cousin led Anthony to seek his fortunes in faraway lands.

The voyage to Persia was the brainchild of the Earl of Essex who probably financed most if not the entire venture. It appears that what Essex had in mind

---

32. Davies, *Elizabethans Errant: The Strange Fortune of Sir Thomas Sherley and His Three Sons,* 79.

33. Sir E. Denison Ross et al., *Anthony Sherley and His Persian Adventures* (London, 1933).

was to unite Shah Abbas with the Christian kings and princes of Europe to halt further advances of the Ottoman Turks in Europe. The plan was for Shah Abbas to launch campaigns in Eastern Anatolia while European princes would move to capture Cypress, thus dividing the Turkish forces. Essex's further objective was for Sherley to ascertain the strength of the Spanish and Portuguese in the Persian Gulf and the volume of their trade. Probably equally important to Essex was to explore commercial opportunities and establish trading links with the Persian court whose tale of riches had reached Europe. This was not the first attempt to engage Persia in Turco-European affairs. In 1592 some seven years before the arrival of the Sherleys, Pope Clement VIII had sent a proposal to Shah Abbas that he and the Christian princes of Europe should combine in a league against the Turks, but Shah Abbas was still occupied with the Uzbeks in the east and was not yet ready to face the enemy to the west.[34]

Sir Anthony and Robert departed England on New Year's Day 1598. Robert was about seventeen at the time. At the beginning of his journey Anthony met a merchant in Venice, Angelo Corrai, who told great tales of Shah Abbas who was "bountiful and liberal to strangers." Corrai offered that he would be glad to be his guide for the trip to Persia. Anthony now hoped

---

34. Davies, *Elizabethans Errant: The Strange Fortune of Sir Thomas Sherley and His Three Sons,* 103–4.

for something more lucrative than a mere diplomatic victory for his patron, Essex. Anthony was already in debt for his previous ventures and he was hoping to be liberally compensated.

They started from Venice: Anthony, Robert, and Angelo Corrai, the volunteer guide and interpreter; Abel Pinçon, a Frenchman who had studied in England; two Englishmen, William Parry and George Manwaring; altogether a party of twenty-six or twenty-seven persons. They embarked at Malmoco, a small port near Venice, on 24 May 1598,[35] taking a boat across the Mediterranean headed for Tripoli and then to Aleppo. There was some hardship as they ran out of food. Anthony spent an unexpectedly large sum of money and "charged Lord Essex for his bills."[36] After a few days of rest they traveled to Mesopotamia then east to Qazvin, which had been the Persian capital during the reign of Shah Tahmasp and had served as the base of operation in the wars with the Ottomans.

When the Sherleys arrived in Qazvin, Shah Abbas had not yet returned from his punitive expedition against the Uzbeks in Khorasan. When the shah arrived the guests were furnished with expensive garments and a magnificent banquet was held in Anthony's honor. The shah invited the Sherleys and their companions to accompany him to Isfahan, the new capital. They were bestowed with substantial gifts.

35. Ibid., 65–66.
36. Ibid., 89.

Shah Abbas issued a farman (court order) granting all Christian merchants in perpetuity the right to trade in all parts of the shah's dominions and freedom to practice their religion.

Anthony stayed less than six months in Persia, from 1 December 1599 to early May 1600. In his accounts he exaggerates what he did for the shah's army, which is mostly fabricated. The time available for any reforms to be effected by a man who never knew a word of Persian or the Turkish dialect of the Safavid court was negligible. Sir Anthony says he was given the cavalry to train and was also commanded to reform and retrain the shah's artillery. It has been said that Anthony introduced canons to the shah's army, but this cannot be true. Since he claimed to have had a commission to retrain the artillery, it must therefore have existed earlier. It is known that prior to Sherley's arrival Uruq Beq (Don Juan of Persia) took part in the siege of Tabriz at which Iranians employed canons.[37]

It has been mentioned by several writers that the Sherleys also taught Persians the use of muskets, but this too is untrue, since Persian infantry carried

---

37. Savory, "The Sherley Myth"; and Uruch Beg (or Uruq Beq), *Don Juan of Persia: A Shia Catholic, 1560–1640*; translated by O. G. Le Strange (Great Britain, 1926). Translated from original Persian, first published in 1604 and republished in Great Britain, 1926. Uruq Beq was the son of a nobleman who was the commander of a regiment and had been killed in battle in 1585 at the Siege of Tabriz. Uruq Beq became the commander of the same regiment after his father's death.

firearms in Uruq Beq's day.[38] George Manwaring who accompanied Anthony to Iran says, "Persians were very good in the use of muskets."[39] Thomas Herbert confirms this.[40] There is no doubt that "Anthony was a rogue."[41]

"The earliest European reference to the use of handguns in Persia can be dated to around 1507, that is about ninety-one years before the arrival of the Sherleys. There are frequent subsequent references to their use, for example in 1520 at Herat and onward.[42] Savory documents that the Portuguese furnished Shah Tahmasp with ten or twenty canons in 1548 at the time of the Ottoman ruler Soleyman the Magnificent's second invasion of Persia. In 1569 Ivan the Terrible sent canons and muskets to Shah Tahmasp.[43]

The origin of the controversy is the fact that the Persians did not use artillery at the key battle of Chaldiran where the Ottomans defeated the Persian army on 22 August 1514 and occupied Tabriz. The single factor in

---

38. Ibid., 110–11.

39. George Manwaring in *True Discourse on Sir Anthony's Travels* quoted by Sir E. Denison Ross in his *Anthony Sherley and His Persian Adventures*, 201.

40. Thomas Herbert, *Some Years Travels into Diverse Parts of Africa and Asia – Particularly the Empires of Persia and Hindustan* (London, 1677).

41. Savory, "The Sherley Myth."

42. Ibid.

43. Roger Savory, *Iran under the Safavids* (Cambridge University, 1980), and "The Sherley Myth."

the defeat was Ottoman artillery supported by hand-guns. "The question arises why did the Safavids not use artillery and handguns at the battle of Chaldiran. The Persians had an innate dislike of firearms, the use of which they considered unmanly and cowardly. In this opinion they were supported by the Mamluks of Egypt and Syria and they disliked artillery which hampered the swift maneuvers of their cavalry."[44]

The Sherleys clearly neither trained nor equipped the Persian army; however, having decided to send an embassy to Europe, the shah selected Sir Anthony as his ambassador or at least as one of the ambassadors. Before leaving Persia on his mission, Sir Anthony corresponded with friends in England. In April he wrote to the Earl of Essex informing him that he was to receive a pension of 30,000 crowns per year from the shah.[45] Shakespeare appears to have closely followed the travels of the Sherleys. *Twelfth Night* has reference to the pension given by the shah.[46]

Uruq Beq became one of the secretaries sent by Shah Abbas to accompany Sir Anthony Sherley in 1599 to European capitals to secure alliances against the Turks. The first embassy was to Boris Godunov in Russia. After some six months in Moscow Anthony

---

44. Ross, *Sir Anthony Sherley and His Persian Adventures*, 163. Savory, "The Sherley Myth."

45. Davies, *Elizabethans Errant: The Strange Fortune of Sir Thomas Sherley and His Three Sons,* 113–14.

46. *Twelfth Night*, II, 5, 80–81.

embarked from Archangel early in 1600 and sailed to Emden in the Netherlands then on to Prague. He had to take the circuitous route as the Ottomans controlled the customary route between Persia and Europe. William Parry had transferred at the coast of Holland to a passing ship going to England and delivered Sir Anthony's letters to Sir Robert Cecil, King James VI of Scotland, and the Earl of Essex. In his letter to King James VI he took credit for having succeeded in separating the Shi'a Persians from the main body of Moslems, something Shah Isma'il had done some ninety years earlier. He also took credit for having persuaded Shah Abbas to unite with the Christians of Europe against the "great enemy of God," the Sultan of Turkey.[47]

In October 1600 Anthony reached Prague where he was received by Emperor Rudolph II. The shah had sent too many people to Europe and each claimed to be the spokesman or ambassador. To the Safavids an ambassador was a person carrying messages from the shah; to the Europeans only one person could be the spokesman for the ruler. The Persians had accused Sherley, probably with some justification, of having sold or given away the gifts Shah Abbas intended for European princes. As disenchantment with Anthony grew most of the Persians accompanying him as sec-

---

47. Davies, *Elizabethans Errant: The Strange Fortune of Sir Thomas Sherley and His Three Sons,* 126–27.

retaries left. Uruq Beq traveled to Spain and converted to Christianity.[48]

From Prague Anthony went to Rome where his fellow ambassador Hoseyn Ali Beq Bayat disassociated himself from Sherley and went on alone to Spain in May 1601. Sir Anthony's fortunes declined from this point. In March 1602 he went to Venice and from there he carried on a correspondence with the king of Spain. Some of his letters were intercepted by English agents and were deemed treasonable. Anybody connected with the recently executed Essex was now suspect. Anthony's request to be allowed to return to England was denied. English ambassadors abroad were instructed to repudiate him.

Financial troubles began to hound Anthony. In mid-1603 he was arrested in Venice and imprisoned either as an insolvent debtor or for sedition. It is not clear what the exact charges were. He was subsequently released and after the accession of James I he was granted a "license" by the English government to "remain beyond the sea somewhat longer."[49] In the spring of 1605 he was sent by Emperor Rudolph to Morocco to report on the state of that country. About the same time he was again granted the status of ambassador

---

48. Uruq Beq, *Don Juan of Persia*. Some sources, including Uruq Beq himself, maintain that the king and queen of Spain selected the name Don Juan for him. Don Juan died without ever returning to Persia.

49. Davies, *Elizabethans Errant: The Strange Fortune of Sir Thomas Sherley and His Three Sons.*

as the joint representative of James I and Philip IV of Spain. Anthony lived on a pension of 3,000 ducats a year from the king of Spain, most of which went to defray his debts. He remained in Madrid in a state of semi-poverty until his death circa 1635.

Anthony and Robert were dissimilar in character. Robert impressed people as a person of integrity. During his long years at the court of Shah Abbas, waiting for news of Anthony, Robert appears to have been useful. He helped in drilling and training new regiments. Later Shah Abbas appointed Robert as Master General and there is some evidence that he commanded a contingent of troops in battle against the Ottomans in 1604 and 1605. Later Robert served in some capacity as an overseer of customs. In February 1608 Robert married Sampsonia, the daughter of a Circassian chieftain. She was nineteen and he was some ten years older. She was baptized by the Carmelites and given the name Teresia.[50]

Anthony's failure to return to Persia or to report on the progress of his mission could have imperiled Robert's status in Isfahan and it says much for Shah Abbas's fairness that he did not let Anthony's behavior influence his esteem for Robert. After a temporary loss of favor, Robert was sent to Europe on a mission nearly ten years after Anthony's departure. Robert's mission was similar to that of his brother. Robert was also asked to find Anthony and report on

50. Ibid., 226.

whether Anthony had accomplished anything. Commentators differ as to the purpose for which Robert was sent abroad.

Robert Sherley left for Europe on 12 February 1608 with his wife Teresia. They traveled by way of the Caspian Sea, up the Volga to Moscow where they overtook another ambassador of Shah Abbas, Ali Qoli Beq, who had left earlier. They had an audience with the tsar. On leaving Moscow Robert went to Krakow, Poland, where he and his entourage and Ali Qoli Beq were well received at the court of Sigismund III. Teresia was left in a convent in Poland. Robert and Ali Qoli Beq proceeded to the seat of the emperor at Prague. Robert was given the title Count Palatine, which had previously been given to his brother. Robert paid off a large debt that Anthony had left behind. He then left Prague for Florence. Robert had problems wherever he went having to settle Anthony's debts.[51]

From Florence Robert traveled to Rome, arriving there in late September. He had an audience with the pope to induce the king of Spain to invade Cyprus, then join with the Persian army in a two-front attack on the Ottomans. Shah Abbas had also asked the pope to persuade the king of Poland to fight the Turks in Wallachia. It appears the pope did not take any steps in either direction but as a consolation made Robert a count. Robert then traveled to Spain, arriving in the first days of January 1610 where he had an audience

51. Ibid.

with the king and queen. One of the letters Robert handed to King Phillip II was from himself and the other from Shah Abbas. Both letters basically said the same thing: The shah urged that the Turks be attacked by way of Aleppo. The Spaniards did nothing about the Persian proposals. It was again obvious that what the Europeans wanted was for the Persians to fight the Ottomans alone and keep them engaged so they would not make further inroads in eastern Europe.

Robert caught up with his brother in Madrid in 1611 living in near poverty. After fruitless recriminations, Robert left Spain. He went to the Low Countries and took a ship to England. He went to Wiston to see his aged father. In London he had a brief audience with King James I. In the following month he had a formal audience and was received as the shah's ambassador. Shortly thereafter Robert returned to Persia.

During Robert's absence Shah Abbas had greatly improved the military position of Persia. Kandahar had been recovered from the Moghuls and a peace treaty had been signed with the Ottomans in 1611. Abbas had recovered the port of Gambaroun from the Portuguese on the mainland and renamed it Bandar Abbas. Robert persuaded the shah to return the Portuguese soldiers who had been taken prisoners at Gambaroun as a peace offering to the Portuguese who still held Hormuz. He set off again for Spain less than a year after his return. The new mission was basically the same as the previous one of 1609–11. Robert left Isfahan on 10 October with a Carmelite father.

The news of Robert's arrival in Spain brought his brother from Granada. On leaving Spain Robert went to Florence and then Rome and was well received by the Duke of Tuscany and the pope. Robert again brought up the issue of a concerted offensive against Ottoman-held territories. As always no one wanted to make the first move. Robert then traveled east to Poland. In December 1623 some twenty months after leaving Spain he unexpectedly appeared in London with his wife.

King James died in March 1625 succeeded by Charles I. There is record of Robert having been received by the new monarch. In 1626 King Charles decided to send a gentleman of the court, Sir Dodmore Cotton, as ambassador to Persia. Cotton was also asked to determine the status of Robert and whether he truly represented the shah of Persia. The East India Company was instructed to transport both Cotton and Sherley to Persia. Cotton, Robert, and retinue reached Isfahan, but the shah was at Ashraf. After a long journey to the shores of the Caspian they reached Ashraf.[52] They received a cold welcome from the shah. Sir Dodmore put forward proposals for trade that Robert had previously raised in England on behalf of Persia. The shah declared that he had known Robert Sherley for many

---

52. Ibid., 274, based on India office documents; Public Record Office.

years and had granted him as many favors as he had to any Persian. Abbas had allied himself with the English to expel the Portuguese from Hormuz and break their power in the Persian Gulf. Although he had assiduously sought their help, he strove to avoid allowing them to get a firm commercial foothold in the country. The shah soon thereafter departed for Qazvin and the Englishmen followed. On the way both Dodmore Cotton and Robert suffered from severe dysentery. Robert died on 13 July 1628. Cotton died ten days after. Shah Abbas lamented Robert's death.

The story of the Sherleys' experiences embodies no inspiration. Neither the books by Anthony Sherley nor his companions touch on Persian, Ottoman, or English social history. Anthony and Robert were typical of a multitude of English and other European travelers to distant lands for commerce or adventure. The Sherleys' travels, however, have been romanticized and exaggerated by succeeding generations of writers, including Iranians. It is undeniable that they played a large part in reintroducing the Elizabethans to Persia.

Shakespeare was interested in the travels of his countrymen. He dealt with or touched upon foreign trade and commerce in several of his plays.[53] He must have read some books and pamphlets on the travels of the Sherleys in particular. In the autumn of 1601 a little book by William Parry was published in London.

---

53. *The Comedy of Errors*; *Love's Labour's Lost*; *The Merchant of Venice*; *Othello*; and *The Tempest*.

Parry had accompanied Sir Anthony from the beginning of his journey. On his return to England he wrote his book that was the first on the travels of the Sherleys to Persia. It is "an account of Sir Anthony's journey from England to Italy and then to Antioch, Aleppo down the Euphrates to Babylon, across the Tigris River into Persian territory to Qazvin, the former capital thence to Isfahan the new capital, the seat of Shah Abbas, the Sophy, then being appointed the special ambassador of the Sophy, he traveled by way of the Caspian Sea to Moscow then up to Archangel through the Baltic he returned to Italy."[54]

G. B. Harrison,[55] a Shakespearean scholar of note, obliquely suggests that the book by Parry includes passages of sufficient similarity to a *Hamlet* soliloquy to indicate that Shakespeare possibly had read the book. Harrison says, "Parry had something to say of travel and the lofty conceptions it breeds." Parry writes:

"To see these resplendent crystalline heavens overcanopying the earth, invested most sumptuously in height of nature's pride with her richest livery, the particularities whereof, were they discredited according to the truth of their nature, it might breed a scruple

---

54. William Parry, *A New and Larger Discourse on the Travels of Sir Anthony Sherley* (London, 1801).

55. G. B. Harrison, *Shakespeare under Elizabeth* (New York, 1933).

in natural man whether man were, for transgressions, ever unimparadised or no."[56]

But to Hamlet in his dejection: "It goes so heavily with my disposition, that this goodly frame the earth, seems to me a sterile promontory, this most excellent canopy, the air, look you this brave, o'erhanging firmament, this majestical roof fretted with golden fire, why it appeareth nothing to me but a foul and pestilent congregation of vapours. What a piece of work is a man, how noble in reason, how infinite in faculty, in form and moving how like a God: The beauty of the world; the paragon of animals. And yet to me, what is this quintessence of dust?" Act II, Sc 2, 267–78.[57]

---

56. Ibid., 277–78, quoting Parry.

57. *Hamlet* was registered in the Stationer's Register on 26 July 1602. The first performance would have been a few months earlier. It is not difficult to assume Shakespeare had read Parry's book published in 1601. There is no consensus about the sequence of some of the plays of Shakespeare. Scholars differ on the date of composition: A.C. Bradley is silent on the date of composition of *Hamlet*.
The more recent books on Shakespeare suggest the following dates: Peter Ackroyd 1601; Michael Wood 1601; The Nielson and Hill edition of Shakespeare 1600–1601; the Pelican Shakespeare 1600.

PERSIAN AND OTHER EASTERN REFERENCES IN SHAKESPEARE'S PLAYS

"Things alien fascinated Shakespeare. His plays abound with references to distant lands, foreign commodities, strange artifacts, and exotic cultures...On stage he represents Moroccan and Russian ambassadors and Caliban the Carib islander. He tells of perfumes of Arabia...and the veils of Indian women...the dynamic process of interaction between the cultures of Rome and Egypt in *Antony and Cleopatra*; the indigenous islander and the colonist in *The Tempest*; white man and Moor in *Othello*."[1]

---

1. Michael Wood, *Shakespeare* (London, 2003), 204–5.

The uses and purposes of Shakespeare's references vary greatly. Some relate to the plot, some to imagery, and some to contemporary interests and attitudes.[2] To augment these references brief commentaries on the plays under review have been included.

THE COMEDY OF ERRORS (1592–94)

One of the earliest of Shakespeare's plays, it is a comedy with elements of farce. The story of identical twins separated as infants during a fierce storm and shipwreck. Shakespeare himself had fathered twins and he will later use twins in *Twelfth Night* (1599–1600), a far superior and more sophisticated play. The setting of *The Comedy of Errors* is affected by the comings and goings of mercantile enterprises. The references to Persia and guilders should be read in that context.[3]

---

2. The sources for the explanatory notes of the quotations are several editions of Shakespeare's works, encyclopedias, and various books listed in the bibliography.

3. There is an Eastern mystic tone to a passage in *The Comedy of Errors:* "I to the world am like a drop of water / That in the ocean seeks another drop / … / So I, to find a mother and a brother / In quest of them, unhappily, lose myself." I, 2, 35–40.
Similar thoughts were expressed earlier by the great Persian lyric poet Sa'di (circa 1184–circa 1291) in his *Bustan:* "A drop of rain fell from a cloud / It was shamed when it saw the vastness of the sea. / Who am I when there is a sea? / If it exists I truly am nothing."

Act IV, Scene 1, Lines 1–6

Merchant: …I am bound

To Persia, and want guilders for my voyage:

Note: Guilders were the coinage of the Netherlands (the Low Countries), which was a maritime power, and likely were used for voyages. Furthermore, Elizabethans probably were not familiar with Persian currency though aware of merchant travelers to that country such as Richard Chancellor and Anthony Jenkinson.

Act IV, Scene 2, Lines 102–4

Antipholus of Ephesus: Give her this key, and tell her, in the desk

That's cover'd o'er with Turkish tapestry

There is a purse of ducets; let her send it.

THE TAMING OF THE SHREW (1593–94)

Baptista Minola, a wealthy man of Padua, has two daughters: Katherine the beautiful elder daughter who is a shrew and given to fits of temper, and Bianca the younger daughter who is gentle and has many suitors. Minola, following tradition, will not allow the younger daughter to marry before her older sister. Petruchio, a handsome eligible young man, has traveled from Verona "to wive it wealthily in Padua." But if he is to marry into the Minola family he must marry Katherine. The play becomes the taming of the shrewish Katherine.

Shakespeare will have both powerful and submissive women in his later plays, but *The Taming of the Shrew* has been singled out as sexist for its portrayal of women in a patrimonial society. The play is not regarded as one of the best of Shakespeare's comedies. It lacks the poetry and the character of a Rosalind as in *As You Like It* or the poetry and sophistication of *Twelfth Night*.

Induction, Scene 2, Lines 37–39

Lord: Or wilt thou sleep? We'll have thee to a couch,

Softer and sweeter than the lustful bed

On purpose trimm'd up for Semiramis.

Note: Semiramis is a legendary Assyrian queen, notoriously voluptuous and lustful.

Act II, Scene 1, Lines 346 and 353

Gremio: First, as you know, my house within the city

Is richly furnished with plate and gold,

…

Fine linen, Turkey cushions boss'd with pearl.

THE TWO GENTLEMEN OF VERONA (1594)

Some scholars believe it is the first play of Shakespeare, written circa 1590–91. The two gentlemen are Valentine (the patron saint of flowers) and Proteus (the sea god of classical mythology). Julia is loved by Proteus and Sylvia is loved by Valentine.

Act II, Scene 6, Lines 25–26

Proteus: …

And Sylvia witness heaven that made her fair

Shows Julia but a swarthy Ethiop.

Note: Julia is dark-haired.

LOVE'S LABOUR'S LOST (1594–95)

Ferdinand, the king of Navarre, decides to devote his remaining years to contemplative endeavors and forego all contact with women. He persuades three of his courtiers to join him. As he is about to embark on this reflective journey, the beautiful princess of France accompanied by three ladies in waiting arrive unexpectedly at his court. The king and his three noblemen fall hopelessly in love and all vows are broken. It is not considered as one of Shakespeare's great plays, but it is popular.

The many references to Russia in the play may be accounted for by the fact that in 1553 a company under the name of "The Mysterie and Company of

Merchant Adventurers for the Discovery of Regions, Dominions, Islands and Places Unknown" had been formed in London to discover a northeast passage to China. After discovery of the route to Archangel in northeast Russia, the company was renamed successively "The Muscovy Company" and "The Russia Company." Most of the ships that set out were lost in storms, but Richard Chancellor went down the Volga River as far as Moscow. Later Anthony Jenkinson reached Archangel, then made it down the Volga to the Caspian Sea and across to Persia. It is the fortitude and bravery of these seamen that Shakespeare praises in the play. (Refer to earlier chapter titled Travelers to Persia and Commercial Relations.)

Act IV, Scene 3, Lines 97, 115–18

Dumaine: Once more I'll read the ode I have writ

…

Thou for whom Jove would swear

Juno but an Ethiop were,

And deny himself for Jove,

Turning mortal for thy love.

Note: Ethiop or black African is intended as a disparagement.

Act IV, Scene 3, Lines 218–24

Berowne: …who sees the heavenly Rosaline,

That like a rude and savage man of Inde,

At the first op'ning of the gorgeous east,

Bows not his vassal head, and strooken blind,

Kisses the base ground with obedient breast?

Act V, Scene 2

Lines 120–21 – Boyet: They…are apparell'd thus,

Like Muscovites or Russians, as I guess.

Note: Russian costumes were not uncommon in English court masquerades.

Lines 302–3 – Rosaline: Let us complain to them what fools were here,

Disguis'd like Muscovites, in shapeless gear.

Line 361 – Princess: A mess of Russians left us but of late.

Lines 392–93 – Rosaline: Help, hold his brow, he'll sound! Why look you so pale?

Sea-sick I think, coming from Muscovy.

Lines 400–1 – Berowne: …

And I will wish thee never more to dance,

Nor never more in Russian habit wait.

A MIDSUMMER NIGHT'S DREAM (1595–96)

The Duke of Athens is to wed Hippolyta, queen of the Amazons, and to celebrate his wedding he has ordered that a grand spectacle be staged. All is not serene in the dukedom. Oberon, the king of the fairies, is quarreling with Titania the queen. There are lovers who lament the absence of their beloveds. There are also a host of comic characters: Quince, the carpenter who is the author of the play to be presented in honor of the duke's wedding, takes himself too seriously. He has named the play "The most lamentable comedy and most cruel death of Pyramus and Thisby." Bottom, the weaver and lead actor in the play, is one of the most endearing characters. There is also the fairy Puck who makes mischief.

Act II, Scene 1, Lines 18–27

Puck: The King doth keep his revels here tonight;

Take heed the Queen come not within his sight;

For Oberon is passing fell and wrath,

Because that she as her attendant hath

A lovely boy stolen from an Indian King;

She never had so sweet a changeling.

Act II, Scene 1, Lines 68–69

Titania (to Oberon): …Why art though here

Come from the farthest steep of India?

Act III, Scene 1, Lines 97–98

Flute: …I'll meet thee, Piramus, at Ninny's tomb.

Quince: "Ninus' tomb," man.

Note: Ninus was the mythical founder of Nineveh; his wife Semiramis reputedly built the city of Babylon, the site of the story of Pyramus and Thisby, which is being enacted.

Act III, Scene 2, Lines 137–38, 140–43

Demetrius: O Helen, goddess, nymph, perfect, devine!

That pure congealed white, high Taurus' snow,

Fanned with the eastern wind, turns to a crow

When thou hold'st up thy hand…

Note: Taurus is a mountain range in Asiatic Turkey that was part of the Persian Empire.

Act III, Scene 2, Line 257

Lysander (to Hermia): Away, you Ethiop!

Act III, Scene 2, Lines 262–64

Hermia: Why are you grown so rude? What change is this sweet love?

Lysander: Thy love? Out, tawny Tartar, out!

Note: Ethiop was used as a disparagement of Hermia's dark coloring; this further ethnic slur is "tawny Tartar", a central Asian Turkic and Mongol people.

Act III, Scene 2, Line 375

Oberon: I'll to my Queen and beg her Indian boy…

Act IV, Scene 1, Lines 53–56

Oberon: And that same dew which sometimes on
the buds

Was wont to swell like round and orient pearls…

THE MERCHANT OF VENICE (1596–97)

In the reign of Edward I (1272–1307) Jews had been officially banished from England. A few remained, mostly in London, but they made a secret of their religion. This is a difficult play in which no one comes out well. Christians are depicted as money-loving, careless, wasteful people and somewhat hedonistic. Shylock, a Jew, is depicted as a suffering loving father but also a vengeful usurer. Shylock has been wronged and humiliated time and again by Christians. Furthermore his daughter Jessica has renounced her faith and eloped with a Christian, Lorenzo. His longtime servant Launcelot has been lured away by his enemies. *The Merchant of Venice* is not an anti-Semitic play as some have suggested. Shylock is arrogant and unforgiving, but the play could be read as dealing with a powerless minority seeking retribution. In 1594, at least two years before Shakespeare's play, there was a trial and execution of Dr. Roderigo Lopez, a prominent Jewish Portuguese physician. Lopez was accused of attempting to poison the queen. The tone of the play was probably influenced by this incident.

The principal romantic male character, Bassanio, has squandered all of his wealth and now in order to marry Portia, a beautiful, intelligent woman with many suitors, appeals to the merchant Antonio for a loan. Antonio, an honorable sort, has his entire fortune tied up in commerce and his goods are on a ship on the high seas. The noble Antonio in order to help his friend Bassanio is forced to borrow money from Shylock.

Shylock insists on the insertion of a vengeful clause in the loan agreement with Antonio that in the event of default the borrower forfeits a pound of flesh. Antonio's ship is lost in a storm and Shylock wants to enforce the contract. The case is decided by Portia who has disguised herself as a judge. She rules wisely that the agreement is unenforceable and Shylock has no recourse.

Portia is a sympathetic character. The two most memorable passages in the play are Shylock's speech in which he asks for tolerance: "Hath not a Jew eyes, Hath not a Jew hands…" (III, 2, 60–76); and Portia's plea: "The quality of mercy is not strain'd. It droppeth as the gentle rain from heaven upon the place beneath…" (IV, 1, 184–205).

The play also has a host of legal implications. There are numerous references to the sanctity of bonds and contracts; the bond of marriage and the bond of friendship. Jessica breaks a filial bond. Launcelot breaks the bond of master and servant, which in sixteenth-century England was inviolable. Then there is the main bond between a lender and borrower, which is unconscionable and hence unenforceable.

Act II, Scene 1, Lines 24–28

> Prince of Morocco: …By this scimitar
>
> That slew the Sophy and the Persian Prince
>
> That won three fields of Sultan Solyman,
>
> I would o'erstate the sternest eyes that look,
>
> Outbrave the heart most daring on the earth…

Note: Safavid shahs were commonly referred to by Western writers as Sophy or Sophi, probably a corruption of the name of the founder of the Safavid order, Sheikh Safi, much like Elizabeth being alluded to as The Tudor and James I as The Stuart.

Sultan Solyman is the Turkish ruler Suleiman II, The Magnificent (1520–66).

Act II, Scene 7, Lines 41–43

> Prince of Morocco: The Hyrcanian deserts and the vasty wilds
>
> Of wide Arabia are as thoroughfares now
>
> For princes to come view fair Portia.

Note: Hyrcania, a province of ancient Persia, is an area southeast of the Caspian Sea, comparable to the current Iranian provinces of Khorasan and Gorgan.

Act III, Scene 2, Lines 97–101

Bassanio: Thus ornament is but the guiled shore

To a most dangerous sea; the beauteous scarf

Veiling an Indian beauty; in a word,

The seeming truth which cunning times put on

To entrap the wisest.

Note: Indian connotes a dark complexion hidden by a veil.

Act III, Scene 2, Lines 268–71

Bassanio: From Tripolis, from Mexico, and
     England

From Lisbon, Barbary, and India,

And not one vessel scape the dreadful touch

Of merchant-marring rocks?

Act IV, Scene 1, Lines 29–33

Duke: Enow to press a royal merchant down,

And pluck commiseration of his state

From brassy bosoms and rough hearts of flints,

From stubborn Turks, and Tartars never train'd

To offices of tender courtesy.

Note: Tartars are Central Asian Turkic and Mongol people.

THE MERRY WIVES OF WINDSOR (1597)

Falstaff, one of the greatest and most lovable of all Shakespeare's characters, appeared in *Henry IV, Parts 1* and *2,* and his death is perfunctorily announced in *Henry V.* Readers have been perplexed as to why Shakespeare resurrected Falstaff in this inferior play. A myth has developed that Queen Elizabeth so loved the character that Shakespeare felt he had to revive him in one or more plays. Sir John Falstaff is now a tame character with very few memorable lines or aphorisms. The great secondary characters of Pistol and Shallow are also witless, although Pistol has a well-known line: "Why the world is my oyster which I with a sword will open" (II, 2, 2–3). There is very little poetry.

Act I, Scene 3, Lines 9–10

Host: Thou'st an emperor – Caesar, Keiser, and Pheazar.

Note: **Pheazar or vizier is from the Arabic/Persian word** *vazir* **meaning "minister."**

Act I, Scene 3, Lines 84 and 88

Pistol: Let vultures gripe thy guts…

Base Phrygian Turk!

Note: **Phrygian Turk is a garbled insult. Phrygia is ancient Troy, now part of Turkey.**

Act II, Scene 1, Lines 144–46

Page: I will not believe such a Cataian, though the priest o' th' town commend him for a true man.

Note: Cataian is a person from Cathay (i.e., China). In Elizabethan times, the truthfulness of the Chinese was questioned.

Act II, Scene 3, Lines 27–30

Host of the Garter Inn (to Doctor Caius): …Is he dead, my Ethiopian? Is he dead, my Francisco? Ha, bully? What says my Aesculapius? My Galien? My heart of elder?

Note: Ethiopian alludes to Doctor Caius' dark complexion; Francisco meaning Frenchman; Aesculapius (Asclepius) the Greek god of medicine; Galien (Galen) the famous Greek physician and medical authority of the second century A.D.

Act IV, Scene 5, Lines 16–21

Host: …Bully – knight! Bully Sir John! Speak from thy lungs military. Art thou there? It is thine host, thine Ephesian, calls.

Falstaff: How now, mine host?

Host: Here's a Bohemian-Tartar tarries the coming down of thy fat woman…

Note: Ephesian possibly implies unruly and loose living. Ephesus was an ancient city of Asia Minor that passed from Lydian control to the Persian Empire.

Bohemian-Tartar is a mixed reference. Bohemia was a kingdom of Central Europe that was in religious turmoil. Tartars are Central Asian Turkic and Mongol people who merged in the invasion of Europe by the Mongols, also known as the Tatar invasion. The name Tatar was first given them in Persia.

MUCH ADO ABOUT NOTHING (1598–99)

Although this play is not on the same level as *As You Like It* or *Twelfth Night*, it is still one of Shakespeare's superior works. It is a tale of the romance and tribulations of two couples. Beatrice is one of Shakespeare's more engaging women. The play also has one of his very amusing characters, Dogberry, a pompous constable. There is a villain, Don John, who is captured and humiliated at the end. He is a forerunner of Iago but not as clever or cunning and all his machinations come to nothing.

Act II, Scene 1, Lines 263–71

Benedick: Will your Grace command me any
    service to the world's end? I will go on the
    slightest errand now to the Antipodes that you
    can devise to send me on; I will fetch you a
    toothpicker now from the furthest inch of Asia,
    bring you the length of Prestor John's foot, fetch
    you a hair of the great Cham's beard, do you any
    embassage to the Pigmies, rather than hold three
    words' conference with this harpy.

Note: **Prester John is a legendary Eastern ruler who was both emperor and Christian priest. Prester is a shortened form of Presbyter (i.e., priest).**

Cham is the khan of Tartary, ruler of the Mongols.

Pigmies were thought at that time to inhabit the mountains of India.

AS YOU LIKE IT (1599)

One of Shakespeare's greatest plays. A French duke is overthrown by his younger brother Frederick and his lands are confiscated. The old duke and a few close members of his court are forced to seek shelter in the forest of Arden. Later Frederick banishes the old duke's daughter Rosalind who also seeks refuge in the forest. The play begins in a corrupt and cruel court but ends in Arden, a heavenly refuge where lovers are united and old enmities are ended. Even Frederick, once he sets foot in Arden with the intention of killing his older brother, is converted to a pious life.

The most original character is Rosalind. She is the life force central to the play and is instrumental in bringing peace and reconciliation to a society that is in turmoil. The play also has two other vital characters, Touchstone the clown and Jacques a cynical observer of the human condition who is a lord attending on the banished Duke. Jacques is remembered for his sardonic but insightful soliloquy on the seven ages of man (II, 7, 139–66).

Act II, Scene 5, Lines 60–61

Jacques: …I'll go to sleep, if I can; if I cannot, I'll rail against all the first born of Egypt.

Note: "First born" suggests the elder of the two dukes (who is banished). The phrase is also a biblical reference, from the account of the death of all first born in Egypt (*Exodus* 11–12).

Act III, Scene 2, Lines 88–95

Rosalind (reading verse written to her by Orlando):

From the east to western Inde, no jewel is like Rosalind.

Her worth, being mounted on the wind,

Through all the world bears Rosalind.

Act IV, Scene 1, Lines 146–53

Rosalind (disguised as a man): …I will be more jealous of thee than a Barbary cock-pigeon over his hen.

Note: Barbary cock-pigeon is a kind of pigeon originally from the Barbary coast of Africa. Pigeons are noted for their monogamy. The term Barbary, however, was also applied to Eastern non-Christians, particularly Moslems, and here refers to the practice by Eastern husbands of secluding their wives from public view.

Act IV, Scene 3, Lines 31–36

Rosalind (reading a letter): Why, 'tis a boisterous and cruel style,

A style for challengers. Why, she defies me,

Like Turk to Christian. Women's gentle brain

Could not drop forth such giant-rude invention,

Such Ethiop words, blacker in their effect

Than in their countenance…

Note: Turks were viewed as a threat to Christian European countries.

TWELFTH NIGHT, OR WHAT YOU WILL (1601–2)

The only play of Shakespeare with an alternate title. "Will" for Elizabethans was wish or inclination. Twelfth Night is the Feast of Epiphany, which is twelve days after Christmas, originally a major Christian feast commemorating the coming of the Magi to Bethlehem. Over the centuries, the pious feast turned into a hedonistic celebration. All attempts by the church to suppress this practice failed. In Shakespeare's lifetime it continued to be a bawdy affair.

Twelfth Night takes place in Illyria, a country on the east coast of the Adriatic Sea. It is one of Shakespeare's great plays and hosts more than the usual number of odd characters. There is Orsino, the sentimental Duke of Illyria who is in love with love. He marries

Viola, who had been masquerading as a man, Cesario. There is Olivia, a wealthy beautiful countess who marries Sebastian, the twin brother of Viola, whom she has just encountered and has fallen in love with him at first sight. Sir Toby Belch, Olivia's uncle, is drunk in every scene and sponges off the generosity of his niece. The wealthy Sir Andrew Aguecheek, probably the most stupid character in all of Shakespeare, lives in the castle as the guest of Sir Toby. Feste the Fool composes and sings some of the most beautiful songs in Shakespeare.

Finally there is the self-satisfied, narcissistic, humorless Malvolio, Olivia's steward. Malvolio is a Puritan but also a social climber who wants to improve his status and marry his employer Olivia. He is easy prey for a prank Viola and Sir Toby devise. Shakespeare is especially hard on him. Sir Toby tells Malvolio, "Dost thou think because thou art virtuous there shall be no more cakes and ale?" (II, 3, 122–25). Shakespeare obviously dislikes religious fundamentalists.

Act I, Scene 2, Lines 62–63

Sea Captain (to Viola): Be you his eunuch, and your mute I'll be,

When my tongue blabs, then let mine eyes not see.

Note: **Both mutes and eunuchs were servants in the Turkish court and harem for obvious reasons.**

Act II, Scene 3, Lines 75–79

Sir Toby Belch: My Lady's a Cataian, we are politicians, Malvolio's a Peg-a-Ramsey, and [sings] "Three merry men be we." Am not I consanguineous? Am I not of her blood? Tilly-vally! Lady! [sings] "There dwells a man in Babylon, lady, lady."

Note: Cataian, a native of Cathay (China), at that time had the meaning of one whose word cannot be trusted.

"There dwells a man in Babylon" is the first line of a popular ballad of the period.

Act II, Scene 3, Line 177

Sir Toby (to Maria): Good night, Penthesilea.

Note: Penthesilea was queen of the Amazons, mythical female warriors of Scythia. This is an allusion to Maria's size. Scythians were an ancient nomadic people of southwestern Asia north of Persia. Their language was of Persian origin.

Act II, Scene 5, Lines 13–14

Sir Toby: …How now,

My metal of India?

Note: Indians used gold decoration extensively in their attire and furnishings.

Act II, Scene 5, Lines 80–81

Sir Toby: I will not give my part of this sport for a
pension of thousands to be paid from the Sophy.

Note: This is a reference to Sir Anthony Sherley (or
Shirley) who in 1599 returned to Europe from a visit to
the shah of Persia (Shah Abbas I) boasting of gifts and
a pension that he said the shah had given him. (See the
section titled The Sherleys).

Act III, Scene 4, Lines 273–79

Sir Toby: ...I had a pass with him, rapier, scabbard,
and all...They say he has been fencer to
the Sophy.

Note: Fencer is one who guards or defends by use of a
sword. The Sophy is the Persian shah (see note on *The
Merchant of Venice* II, 1, 24–28).

Act IV, Scene 2, Lines 42–44

Clown: Madman, thou errest. I say there is no
darkness but ignorance, in which thou art more
puzzled than the Egyptians in their fog.

Note: In Exodus 10:22 Moses brought a three-day fog
on the Egyptians.

Act V, Scene 1, Lines 117–20

Duke: Why should I not, had I the heart to do it,

Like to th' Egyptian thief at point of death,

Kill what I love? – a savage jealousy

That sometimes savors nobly...

Note: This comparison refers to an episode of the *Ethiopica* of Heliodorus in which Thyamis, an Egyptian robber captain, who when in great danger attempts to kill his mistress rather than let her fall into the hands of his enemies.

TROILUS AND CRESSIDA (1601–2)

A play with relevance to the twentieth century. The death of honor and chivalry. The Trojan War is a savage and sordid marital quarrel. Shakespeare's recounting of it is by no means romantic or chivalrous. It is a dark and cynical view of human nature. There are no heroes and everyone is flawed. Ulysses is merely a crafty politician. Achilles is too proud and Ajax is dim-witted. The war could have come to an end if the Trojans had accepted the Greek offer to return Helen and pay an indemnity.

Act I, Scene 3, Lines 327–31

Nestor: …But that Achilles, were his brain as barren

As banks of Libya, though, Apollo knows,

'Tis dry enough…

ALL'S WELL THAT ENDS WELL (1602–3)

Bertram, young Count of Rossillion, and his useless and parasitic companion Parolles travel to the court of France and offer their services. He leaves his mother the Countess of Rossillion and her ward the beautiful orphan Helena, the daughter of a famous physician. Helena, who is in love with Bertram, follows him to the French court. The king is sick with an incurable disease. Helena makes a bargain with the king. If she were to cure him, she could select a husband from among his courtiers. She uses a prescription her late father had used for a similar ailment and the king is cured. Helena chooses Bertram who refuses and pleads with the king that she is of low rank. Although Helena retracts her demand, the king forces Bertram to wed her. The play covers the journey of Helena and Bertram and their ultimate reconciliation.

Act IV, Scene 1, Lines 41–43

Parolles: …Tongue, I must put you into a butter-
woman's mouth and buy myself another of
Bajazeth's mule, if you prattle me into
these perils.

Note: **Bajazeth is a Turkish name. Some editors amend
"mule" to "mute" citing *Henry V* (I, 2, 232): "Like Turkish
mute, shall have a tongueless mouth..."**

MEASURE FOR MEASURE (1604)

The title of this great play derives from the Sermon on the Mount. "With what you mete, it shall be measured to you again." A very dark but a great play where base human nature is exposed. The play, however, has a most unsatisfactory ending.

Vincente the Duke of Vienna is planning to travel and leaves the city in the hands of his deputy Angelo. The deputy revives an old discarded law imposing the death penalty for fornication. He makes an example of Claudio, a young man who has made Juliet, with whom he has a betrothal contract, pregnant. When Claudio's chaste sister who is about to enter a convent pleads for her brother's life, Angelo is smitten by her. He offers to free Claudio if she would offer sexual favors to him. The duke hears of Angelo's machinations and returns to Vienna in disguise. He chastises Angelo but nevertheless keeps him in his lofty position though he is humiliated; Claudio is pardoned and completes the marriage rites with Juliet.

Almost all of Shakespeare's plays end with the introduction of a new order. Here nothing changes and Angelo could wreak havoc again.

Act III, Scene 2, Lines 88–89

Lucio: Some say he is with the Emperor of Russia; other some, he is in Rome; but where is he, think you?

Note: In the sixteenth century English travelers had found a northeast route to Persia from Archangel south through Russia and after having been received by the tsar down across the Caspian Sea (see chapter titled Travelers to Persia and Commercial Relations).

THE FIRST PART OF HENRY THE SIXTH (1589–90)

The three parts of *Henry VI* are episodic and begin with his troubled reign. Henry came to the throne as a child and had no chance to be trained in kingship. When he reaches maturity his court is ruled by noblemen of different factions. England is still at war with France and has been defeated badly at Orleans by the French led by Joan La Pucelle (called Joan of Arc) whom the English regard as a sorceress.

Parts II and III cover the War of the Roses and Henry's defeat at St. Albans; the machinations of the Duke of York to install his son Richard, the principal warrior of the York faction, on the throne; the barbarism shown by both sides; the murder of Henry VI and the ultimate assumption of the throne by Richard of York.

Act I, Scene 2, Lines 129–30, 140–41

Joan La Pucelle (Joan of Arc): Assign'd am I to be the English scourge.

This night the siege assuredly I'll raise...

Charles (Dauphin and afterward King of France):
   Was Mahomet inspired with a Dove?

Thou with an eagle art inspired then.

Note: The Prophet of Islam was said in Christian legend to have been inspired by a dove whispering in his ear.

Act I, Scene 3, Lines 38–41

Henry Beauford, Bishop of Winchester, later
   Cardinal: Nay, stand thou back, I will not budge
   a foot:

This be Damascus, be thou cursed Cain,

To slay thy brother Abel, if thou wilt.

Note: In medieval legend Damascus was believed to have been the site where Cain murdered Abel.

Act I, Scene 5, Lines 21–22

Lord Talbot:…A witch by fear, not force,
   like Hannibal,

Drives back our troops and conquers as she lists…

Note: According to the historian Livy, Hannibal, the Carthaginian general, routed the Romans by tying flaming bundles of twigs to the horns of oxen and driving them into the terrified Roman lines.

Act I, Scene 6, Lines 17–27

Charles: 'Tis Joan, not we, by whom the day is won

   …

A statelier pyramis to her I'll rear

Than Rhodope's of Memphis ever was.

In memory of her when she is dead,

Her ashes, in an urn more precious

Than the rich-jewell'd coffer of Darius,

Transported shall be at high festivals

Before the Kings and Queens of France.

Note: "Pyramis" is meant to be "pyramid."

Rhodope was a Greek courtesan who is said to have married the Egyptian king who built a beautiful pyramid to her in Memphis, an ancient city on the Nile.

Alexander the Great defeated the Persian king Darius III. According to legend he took from him a jeweled treasure chest in which Alexander placed his most valued possession, the poems of Homer that he carried on his military campaigns.

Act II, Scene 3, Lines 4–6

Countess of Auvergne: The plot is laid.

If all things fall out right,

I shall as famous be by this exploit

As Scythian Tomyris by Cyrus' death.

Note: Tomyris was a Scythian queen who, according to a legend, killed Cyrus the Great in war and preserved his head in a wineskin filled with blood. Cyrus was the king (sixth century B.C.) who founded the Persian Achaemenid Empire.

Act IV, Scene 7, Lines 72–74

Joan La Pucelle: Here's a silly stately style indeed:

The Turk that two and fifty kingdoms hath,

Writes not so tedious a style as this.

Note: The Turk referred to is the "Grand Turk," the sultan.

THE THIRD PART OF HENRY THE SIXTH (1590–91)

Act I, Scene 4, Lines 113–15, 154–55

Duke of York (to Queen Margaret): How ill-
  beseeming is it in thy sex

To triumph like an Amazonian trull

Upon their woes whom fortune captivates.

…

But you are more inhuman, more inexorable,

O, ten times more, than tigers of Hyrcania.

Note: The Amazons were a race of legendary Greek or
Scythian female warriors. (See note on *Twelfth Night,* II,
4, 177.)

Hyrcania was a province of ancient Persia noted for its
fierce tigers. (See note on *The Merchant of Venice,* II, 7,
41–43.)

Act III, Scene 1, Lines 62–63

King Henry: My crown is in my heart, not on my head;

Not deck'd with diamonds and India stones…

THE TRAGEDY OF RICHARD THE THIRD (1592–93)

There are two famous hunchbacks in world literature: Victor Hugo's hunchback of Notre Dame is kind, loving, and derives pleasure from playing the cathedral bells. And there is the Duke of Gloucester, later Richard III, king of England, a diabolic figure who kills friends and children. He knows he is hated but he revels in that hatred. "If I die no soul shall pity me" (V, 3, 201). Cruelty is rooted in his nature and his twisted body signifies his corrupted mind. He is not as complex a villain as *Othello*'s Iago nor the embodiment of evil as Edmund, Goneril, and Regan in *King Lear*.

The play ends with the killing of Richard at Bosworth Field by the Earl of Richmond, later Henry VII. Richmond marries Elizabeth of York uniting the White Rose of York and the Red Rose of Lancaster, putting an end to the fraternal civil War of the Roses.

Act IV, Scene 4, Lines 321–22

King Richard: …

The liquid drops of tears that you shed

Shall come again, transform'd to orient pearls…

Note: The most beautiful pearls then known were from the Orient.

THE TRAGEDY OF KING RICHARD THE SECOND (1595)

King Richard II, the grandson of Edward III, is extravagant and has emptied the treasury. His incompetence is shown at the very outset. Instead of settling a dispute between Bolingbroke, his cousin and son of the revered John of Gaunt, and Thomas Mowbray, the Duke of Norfolk, he banishes them to exile and seizes the property of Bolingbroke who comes back, organizes an army, topples Richard, and assumes the throne as Henry IV. Richard is murdered at the direction of Bolingbroke.

One of Shakespeare's most engaging plays. Richard II is vastly different from King Richard III. Richard II is neither a monster nor a fool. Richard II, though obviously flawed, is an interesting poet. He appears to enjoy his suffering, which inspires him to create beautiful poetry.

The play abounds with some of Shakespeare's most moving poetry. One of its memorable passages is Richard's lamenting the loss of his throne (III, 3, 143–54).

There is also the oration of John of Gaunt, Henry's aging father near death, the very embodiment of political morality reciting a most stirring song of praise for England (II, 1, 40–50, 65–66):

This royal throne of kings, this sceptered isle,

This earth of majesty, this seat of Mars,

This other Eden, this demi-paradise,

This fortress built by Nature for herself

Against infection and the hand of war,

This happy breed of men, this little world,

This precious stone set in the silver sea,

Which serves it in the office of a wall

Or as a moat defensive to a house

Against the envy of less happier lands,

This blessed plot, this earth, this realm, this
    England…

Act I, Scene 3, Lines 294–97

Bolingbroke: O, who can hold a fire in his hand

By thinking on the frosty Caucasus?

Or cloy the hungry edge of appetite

By bare imagination of a feast?

Note: The Caucasus is a series of mountain ranges between the Black Sea and the Caspian Sea.

Act IV, Scene 1, Lines 134–41

Bishop of Carlisle: My Lord of Hereford here,
    whom you call king,

Is a foul traitor to proud Hereford's King,

And if you crown him, let me prophesy,

The blood of English shall manure the ground,

And future ages groan for this foul act.

Peace shall go sleep with Turks and infidels…

Note: Turks were conquerors and the dreaded foe of Eastern Europe and Persia.

Act V, Scene 5, Lines 76–79

Groom to King Richard: O how it yearn'd my heart
    when I beheld

In London streets, that coronation-day,

When Bolingbroke rode on roan Barbary,

That horse that thou so often hast bestrid…

Note: The name Barbary refers to the pirate coast of North Africa (i.e., Tunisia, Algeria, and Morocco).

THE FIRST PART OF HENRY THE FOURTH (1596–97)

The play opens with a guilt-ridden Henry IV who is planning a pilgrimage to the Holy Land to atone for his sin of regicide (the order to kill Richard II). He has yet to secure his throne. There are rebellions in areas near the Scottish border by the Earl of Northumberland and his son Henry Percy, named Hotspur. There is also rebellion by the Welsh grandee Owen Glendower who has joined Northumberland. Henry delays his pilgrimage to attend to the rebels and the insurrection. King Henry's son, Prince Hal (later Henry V), spends his time in taverns with Sir John Falstaff and his gang. The play is about the transformation of the errant prince into a brave, wise man and his ascendance to the throne upon the death of his father.

There are marvelous characters. The impatient, tempestuous, and brave Hotspur is slain by Prince Hal in man-to-man combat. His last words are especially moving: "O, Harry thou hast robbed me of my youth" (V, 4, 77). There is the near-mad Glendower who believes he can communicate with the dead.

There is also the introduction of the incomparable Falstaff, one of the very greatest creations of Shakespeare and a most lovable character. At Shrewsbury when Prince Hal sees him idle in the midst of the crucial battle, he says to him, "Why, thou owest God a death," and leaves. Falstaff's short soliloquy best describes the absurdity of the belief that wars are honorable and one's manhood is best honed in warfare.

Falstaff has no use for the absurdities and senseless-
ness of chivalry and war (V, 1, 129–39):

> 'Tis not due yet; I would be loathe to pay him
> before his day. What need I be so forward with
> him that calls not on me? Well, 'tis no matter;
> honour pricks me on. Yea, but how if honour
> prick me off when I came on? How then? Can
> honour set a leg? No. An arm? No. Or take away
> the grief of a wound? No. Honour hath no skill
> in surgery, then? No. What is honour? A word.
> What is in that word honour? What is that
> honour? Air; a trim reckoning! Who hath it? He
> that died o' Wednesday. Doth he feel it? No. Doth
> he hear it? No. 'Tis insensible then? Yea, to the
> dead. But will it not live with the living? No.

Act II, Scene 4, Lines 384–87

> Falstaff: …give me a cup of sack to make my eyes
> look red, that it may be thought I have wept, for
> I must speak in passion, and I will do it in King
> Cambyses' vein.

Note: Cambyses was a king of Persia (sixth century
B.C.), son of Cyrus the Great, founder of the Persian
Empire. In "King Cambyses' vein" is an old-fashioned
ranting style like Thomas Preston's *Cambyses*, an early
Elizabethan play.

Act III, Scene 1, Lines 163–67

Mortimer: In faith, he is a worthy gentleman,

Exceedingly well read and profited

In strange concealments, valiant as a lion,

And wondrous affable, and as bountiful

As mines of India……..

Act V, Scene 3, Lines 44–47

Falstaff: O Hal, I prithee give me leave to breathe a while. Turk Gregory never did such deeds in arms as I have done this day. I have paid Percy, I have made him sure.

Note: To the Europeans, Turk denoted a merciless person. Gregory refers either to Pope Gregory VII, who was renowned for violence, or Pope Gregory XIII (1572–85), enemy of England and instigator of the Saint Bartholomew's Day massacre in France in 1572.

THE SECOND PART OF KING HENRY THE FOURTH (1598)

Part I ends with Prince Hal redeeming himself by his valor and saving his father's kingdom. In Part II, the transformation of a wayward son into a fully competent king is complete. There is reconciliation between Hal and his father at the king's deathbed.

Shakespeare is sentimental about the past and many of his good people come from that era (i.e., Falstaff and his crowd). But Henry IV and V are calculating and cold characters. At the end of the play when poor Falstaff has come to praise his protégé, now King Henry V, the king callously turns him away and tells him, "I know thee not old man, fall to thy prayers. How ill white hairs become a fool and jester. (V, 5, 1–52). In inserting that short scene Shakespeare has tarnished the image of Henry V, the hero of Agincourt for modern readers.

Although *Henry IV, Part II* has its share of memorable characters – Bardolph, Pistol, Justices Shallow and Silence, Mistress Quickly, and Doll Tearsheet – *Henry IV Part I* is superior.

Introduction, Lines 1–5

Rumour: I, from the orient to the drooping west,

Making the wind my post-horse, still unfold

The acts commenced on this ball of earth.

Act II, Scene 2, Lines 146–50

Prince: Where sups he? Doth the old boar feed in the old frank?

Bardolph: At the old place, my lord, in Eastcheap.

Prince: What company?

Page: Ephesians, my lord, of the old church.

Note: For Ephesians see note on *The Merry Wives of Windsor,* IV, 5, 16–21.

Act II, Scene 4, Lines 163–67

Pistol: Shall pack-horses

And hollow pamper'd jades of Asia,

Which cannot go but thirty miles a day,

Compare with Caesars and with Cannibals

And Troiant Greeks?…

Note: These lines are a mangled quotation from Christopher Marlowe's *Tamburlaine*. "Cannibals" is an error; the word should be "Hannibals," in reference to the famous Carthaginian general. Troiant Greeks are Trojan Greeks.

Act III, Scene 2, Lines 307–8

Falstaff: …Duer paid to the bearer than the Turk's tribute…

Note: The Turk's tribute is the annual payment collected from merchants by the sultan.

Act V, Scene 2, Lines 47–49

Prince: …This is the English, not the Turkish court,

Not Amurath an Amurath succeeds,

But Harry Harry…

Note: Amurath is Murad III, the Turkish sultan. Legend has it that on his accession to the throne in 1574 he strangled his five brothers.

Act V, Scene 3, Lines 99–101

Pistol: I speak of Africa and golden joys.

Falstaff: O base Assyrian knight, what is
    thy news?…

Note: In this context, Assyrian means alien or pagan.

THE LIFE OF HENRY THE FIFTH (1599)

Shakespeare's early popularity rested a great deal on his history plays, especially the Hundred Years Wars with France, as it brought back memories of victories at Agincourt and Crecy, and the warrior king Henry V.

Henry V is the most jingoistic of Shakespeare's plays. Patriotism has become a religion. At the end of *Henry IV, Part II* the dying but still astute politician Henry IV on his deathbed advises his son, the future king Henry V, "to busy giddy minds / with foreign quarrels…" (IV, 5, 213–16), an age-old device to divert the attention of the citizenry even used in modern times and still today. Young Henry V takes this advice and begins a war with France using the specious argument that England merely wants to reclaim lands in France that had belonged to her. The war becomes justified and England becomes united in pursuit of this claim.

There is a moving and ingenious scene that shows a more humane side of Henry who begins to have trepidations on the eve of the battle of Agincourt, saying, "I and my bosom must debate a while" (IV, 1, 31). He goes out in disguise to where the soldiers are camped and engages them in conversation. In attempting to allay their doubts and fears he strengthens his own resolve.

Act I, Scene 2, Lines 230–33

King Henry: …Either our history shall with full mouth

Speak freely of our acts, or else our grave,

Like Turkish mute, shall have a tongueless mouth,

Not worshipp'd with a waxen epitaph…

Note: For Turkish mutes see note on *Twelfth Night*, I, 2, 62–63.

Act III, Scene 1, Lines 17–21

King Henry: …On, on, you noblest English,

Whose blood is fet from fathers of war-proof!

Fathers that, like so many Alexanders,

Have in these parts from morn till even fought,

And sheath'd their swords for lack of argument.

Note: Alexander the Great wanted further wars and regretted that he had no more worlds to conquer.

Act III, Scene 7, Lines 143–46

Duke of Orleans: Foolish curs, that run winking into the mouth of a Russian bear, and have their heads crush'd like rotten apples! You may as well say, that's a valiant flea that dare eat his breakfast on the lip of a lion.

Note: Russians became known for performing with their ferocious bears.

Act IV, Scene 7, Lines 58–62

King Henry: …If they will fight with us, bid them come down,

Or void the field; they do offend our sight.

If they'll do neither, we will come to them,

And make them skirt away, as swift as stones

Enforced from the old Assyrian slings…

Note: Assyria was an ancient empire of southwestern Asia, governing large areas including Egypt and Babylon. Its most prominent feature was its military prowess.

THE LIFE OF KING HENRY THE EIGHTH
(1612–13)

A disjointed play where a succession of personages appear, some very briefly: the king, Cardinal Wolsey, the Duke of Buckingham, Cranmer the archbishop of Canterbury. The only person who comes alive is Queen Katherine who is to be divorced. The play covers more than twenty years of the reign of Henry VIII from circa1520 to 1544 with Shakespeare manipulating the chronology as in some of his other history plays.

Henry VIII is Shakespeare's final play. Most scholars believe the date of composition to be early 1613. We know the Globe theatre, the home of Shakespeare's plays, was destroyed by fire on June 29, 1613. It is generally accepted that the play is not entirely Shakespeare's and two or three other playwrights may have had a hand in it.

Act I, Scene 1, Lines 18–22

Duke of Norfolk: …Today the French,

All cliquant, all in gold, like heathen gods,

Shone down the English; and, tomorrow, they

Made Britain India: every man that stood

Show'd like a mine…

Note: Britain would seem as rich and elaborate as India, with its mines of gold and shining precious stones, some of which had been brought to England by the East India Company, which had been established in 1600 by Queen Elizabeth.

THE TRAGEDY OF TITUS ANDRONICUS (1593–94)

This is Shakespeare's first attempt at tragedy. It is a weak play modeled on *The Spanish Tragedy* by Thomas Kyd, which had been the rage of London a few years earlier. Despite its Roman setting it is a "revenge play," which was popular in the latter Elizabethan era. The play opens and ends in violence and savagery. There is murder, rape, mutilation, and even cannibalism. It is the story of Titus, a Roman general who is victorious over the Goths. The crown of emperor is offered to him, but he declines. He has brought back as a prized prisoner Tamora, queen of the Goths, who together with Aaron her Moorish lover, exacts her revenge. Titus himself is far from being a hero. He too commits unspeakable acts.

Frank Kermode, an eminent Shakespearean scholar, maintains that it was essential for Shakespeare to try his hand at tragedy in order to firmly establish himself as a playwright and it was inevitable that his great tragedies would follow soon thereafter.

Act II, Scene 1, Lines 9, 15–17, 22–23

Aaron: Hast prisoner held, fett'red in amorous chains,

And faster bound to Aaron's charming eyes

Than is Prometheus tied to Caucasus…

This goddess, this Semiramis, this nymph,

This siren that will charm Rome's Saturnine...

Note: Prometheus was a titan who stole fire from heaven to help mankind. As punishment, Zeus chained him to a peak in the Caucasus, which the ancient world as well as the Elizabethans believed to hold the highest mountains.

Semiramis was an Assyrian queen noted for her beauty and sexuality.

Act II, Scene 3, Lines 72–74

Bassianus: Believe me, Queen, your swart Cimmerian

Doth make your honor of his body's hue,

Spotted, detested, and abominable.

Note: A swart Cimmerian is a swarthy person. The Cimmerians were an ancient people who swept across Asia Minor and are mentioned in Assyrian inscriptions regarding their war. Homer says they lived in a land of darkness.

THE TRAGEDY OF ROMEO AND JULIET (1595–96)

Probably the most popular of Shakespeare's plays, but somehow it lacks the depth of the later great tragedies. By mere misunderstanding and chance the protagonists take their own lives which runs counter to the tradition of classical tragedy. But the play has great emotional intensity and some moving poetry (II, 2, 109–11, 114–16):

Juliet: O swear not by the moon, the inconstant
   moon,

That monthly changes in her circled orb,

Lest that thy love prove likewise variable.

…

Do not swear at all;

Or if thou wilt, swear by thy gracious self,

Which is the god of my idolatry,

And I'll believe thee.

Another of Juliet's beautiful emotional speeches was quoted by the late Robert Kennedy in his eulogy for his brother, President John Kennedy (III, 2, 21–25):

Give me my Romeo, and when (he) shall die,

Take him and cut him out in little stars,

And he will make the face of heaven so fine

That all the world will be in love with night,

And pay no worship to the garish sun.

Act I, Scene 4, Lines 4–6

Benvolio: …We'll have no cupid hoodwink'd with
   a scarf,

Bearing a Tartar's painted bow of lath,

Scaring the ladies like a crow-keeper…

Note: The Tartar archers of Central Asia were said to have used a shorter and more curved bow than the English longbow, formed much like Cupid's lip-shaped bow.

Act I, Scene 5, Lines 44–47

Romeo: O, she doth teach the torches to burn bright!

It seems she hangs upon the cheek of night

As a rich jewel in an Ethiop's ear –

Beauty too rich for use, for earth too dear!

THE TRAGEDY OF HAMLET, PRINCE OF DENMARK (1600–1601)

Shakespeare's *Hamlet* together with Dante's *Divine Comedy* and Goethe's *Faust* are considered high among the seminal works of Western literature. On the surface it appears as another Elizabethan revenge play, but it transcends any category or classification. It is the most performed play of Shakespeare and has been translated into almost all languages. Every ambitious or established actor aspires to play the title role. It has become a yardstick by which great actors are judged. Hamlet is probably the most complex character in all of Shakespeare, lending himself to various interpretations. He has been variously interpreted as being tormented by Oedipal guilt, which prevents him from taking any action as in Laurence Olivier's 1948 film; as an aggressive uninhibited man who bides his time to take revenge as in Nicol Williamson's stage role; and the Soviet film production of a Hamlet who is chiefly concerned with power politics.

Hamlet is by nature cerebral and reflective. When he first comes on the scene he laments, "The time is out of joint. O cursed spirit that I was born to set it right" (I, 5, 191–92). When he becomes convinced that his father had been murdered by his brother Claudius there is little he can do. If he were to kill Claudius he would be branded a murderer and punished. Hamlet wants witnesses and public justice. He wants everyone to know his uncle is corrupt and a murderer. Claudius is crafty and is one of the more urbane of Shakespeare's villains. At play's end two families are destroyed: Polonius, the Lord Chamberlain, his daughter Ophelia and son Laertes; Hamlet, his mother and uncle are also gone. However, as in all of Shakespeare's plays order is restored at the end. Fortinbras, the prince of Norway, will rule Denmark.

The play has some of Shakespeare's loveliest poetry. At the very outset, "But look, the morn, in russet mantle clad walks o'er the due of yon high eastern hill" (I, 2, 166–67). The poetic and deeply emotional soliloquies are well known the world over.

Act II, Scene 2, Lines 435–39

Hamlet: …for the play, I remember, pleas'd not the millions, 'twas caviary to the general…

Note: In the plays "the general" are the common people. Like caviar brought from Persia and Russia, too luxurious for the multitude.

Act II, Scene 2, Lines 445–50

Hamlet (to players): …One speech in't I chiefly lov'd, 'twas Aeneas' tale to Dido, and thereabout of it especially when he speaks of Priam's slaughter. If it live in your memory, begin at this line – let me see, let me see:

"The rugged Pyrrhus, like th' Hyrcanian beast…"

Note: Hyrcania, province of ancient Persia. (see *note on The Merchant of Venice*, II, 7, 39–43)

Act III, Scene 2, Lines 1–4, 12–14

Hamlet (to player): Speak the speech, I pray you, as I pronounc'd it to you, trippingly on the tongue, but if you mouth it, as many of our players do, I had as lief the town-crier spoke my lines…I would have such a fellow whipt for o'erdoing Termagant, it out-Herods Herod, pray you avoid it.

Note: Termagant in medieval drama was mistakenly identified as a god of the Saracens. He was portrayed as noisy and violent.

Act III, Scene 2, Lines 275–78

Hamlet: Would not this, sir, and a forest of feathers – if the rest of my fortunes turn Turk with me

– with two Provincial roses on my raz'd shoes,
get me a fellowship in a cry of players?

Note: To turn Turk means to turn bad.

THE TRAGEDY OF OTHELLO, THE MOOR OF VENICE (1604)

A play about sexual jealousy that destroys a noble man and his innocent wife. It is not about a struggle for control of a state nor the decline of a ruling king as in most of Shakespeare's tragedies. The play is simply constructed although there are several rich subplots. In many ways it is the most dramatic among Shakespeare's works and the action is compressed in time.

Shakespeare had used a Moor as a character in *Titus Andronicus* who is an outright villain. In *Othello* the Moor is a noble person: "That lov'd not wisely but too well; of one not easily jealous, but being wrought and perplexed in the extreme" (V, 2, 344–46). Othello is probably African of high descent who had been converted to Christianity. It was daring of Shakespeare to have a strangely foreign character as the hero of the play.

Othello is charged with the defense of Cyprus against the Ottoman Turks who ruled from Arabia to Egypt, the rest of North Africa, and Eastern Europe to the gates of Vienna. The early scenes show Othello as a capable and brave commander of great integrity. Iago, an officer serving under Othello, is bypassed and Cassio is appointed as Othello's lieutenant. Iago's seething hatred of Othello has its roots there. We learn later from Iago's soliloquy that he begins to believe that Othello has been intimate with his wife Emilia. Thereafter Iago plans Othello's destruction.

Othello is no match for the cunning Iago who together with Edmund in King Lear are among the most villainous characters in world literature. Othello's wife, Desdemona, the daughter of Brabantio a Venetian senator, is the very essence of innocence but Iago has poisoned Othello's mind against her. When too late Iago has been exposed, Othello comes to believe that Iago must be the incarnation of the devil: "I look down toward his feet; but that is a fable. If thou be'st the devil, I cannot kill thee" (V, 2, 288). Othello refers to the belief that the devil had cloven hooves.

Act I, Scene 1 and Act II, Scenes 1, 2, and 3

There are approximately twenty-five references to Turks, Turkish, Ottoman, and Ottomites.

Act III, Scene 3, Lines 453–56

Othello: …Like to the Pontic Sea,

Whose icy current and compulsive course

Nev'r feels retiring ebb, but keeps due on

To the Propontic and the Hellespont…

Note: The Pontic Sea is now the Black Sea. Over the centuries its shores have been occupied by Greeks, Turks, and Tartars.

The Hellespont is now the Dardanelles, straits belonging to Turkey.

Act III, Scene 4, Lines 55–56

Othello: …that handkerchief

Did an Egyptian to my mother give…

Act IV, Scene 2, Lines 224–25

Iago: …He goes into Mauritania and taketh away
with him the fair Desdemona…

Note: Mauritania was a northwest African realm named for the Mauri, a people of Berber, Moorish, and Arab extraction. In the eighth century they became Moslems.

Act IV, Scene 3, Lines 38–39

Emilia: I know a lady in Venice would have walk'd
barefoot to Palestine for a touch of his nether lip.

Act V, Scene 2, Lines 342–56

Othello: Speak of me as I am; nothing extenuate,

Nor set down aught in malice. Then must you speak

Of one that lov'd not wisely but too well;

Of one not easily jealous, but being wrought,

Perplexed in the extreme; of one whose hand

Like the base Indian threw a pearl away

Richer than all his tribe; of one whose subdu'd eyes

Albeit unused to the melting mood,

Drops tears as fast as the Arabian trees

Their medicinable gum. Set you down this;

And say besides, that in Aleppo once,

Where a malignant and a turban'd Turk

Beat a Venetian and traduc'd the state,

I took by th' throat the circumcised dog,

And smote him – thus.

Note: In the text, "base Indian" relates to the idea that Indians were ignorant of the value of their precious possessions. A few editors prefer to read "base Judean," an allusion to Judas Iscariot or to Herod who in a fit of jealousy killed his wife.

Arabian trees' medicinable gum is myrrh, a small tree native to Ethiopia and Arabia from whose stem a yellow gum oozes that is used as an antiseptic, stimulant, and tonic.

Aleppo, now in northwest Syria, was a great Ottoman commercial center.

Circumcised dog is used to denigrate a Moslem rite.

THE TRAGEDY OF KING LEAR (1605)

A tale of a father, Lear, king of Britain, with a kind and caring daughter Cordelia and two monstrous elder daughters, Goneril and Regan. There is a subplot of another father, the Earl of Gloucester, with a kind son Edgar and a demonic younger son Edmund, a bastard who rivals and even surpasses *Othello*'s Iago. Both Cordelia and Edgar are ultimately banished by their respective aged and foolish fathers.

Lear, four score in years, childishly decides to retire and divide his kingdom amongst his three daughters. The size of the gift will depend on each daughter's declaration of love for him. The two elder daughters, Goneril and Regan, shower their father with protestations of unlimited love and praise. Cordelia, the youngest, who truly loves him and has been his favorite, limits herself to a more modest and sincere declaration of duty and affection. The near senile Lear banishes Cordelia and divides his kingdom between the two elder daughters. When the Earl of Kent, his faithful courtier, admonishes Lear, he too is exiled. Goneril and Regan subsequently humiliate their father and finally banish him to the wilderness. The Fool, his only companion, speaks up and says, "I would have you beaten for being old before your time."

There is more hate in *King Lear* than in any Shakespearean family. The ice-blooded Edmund is probably the most evil person in all of Shakespeare. There is the blinding of Gloucester by his bastard son, and the murder of Cordelia. With the exception of Cordelia, Edgar, Kent, and the Duke of Albany there is a dearth of decent people. Lear had been an authoritarian king, uncaring of his people, but both he and Gloucester learn through adversity – only too late. The last scene of the play with the murder of Cordelia and the Fool is one of the most wrenching scenes in all literature.

The play is much more than the ingratitude of children. It questions justice and the existence of a caring God. After Gloucester has been blinded he murmurs, "As flies to wanton boys, we are to the gods, they kill us for their sport" (IV, 2, 39–40).

Act I, Scene 1, Lines 113–19

Lear (to Cordelia): …The barbarous Scythian,

Or he that makes his generation messes

To gorge his appetite, shall to my bosom

Be as well neighbor'd, pitied, and reliev'd

As thou my sometime daughter.

Note: Scythian refers to a member of a tribe (seventh to first century B.C.) that occupied the area roughly from the Black Sea to the Caspian Sea. They were known as barbarians in classical times.

Act III, Scene 4, Lines 90–92

Edgar: …Wine loved I deeply, dice dearly; and in woman out-paramour'd the Turk.

Note: He had more lovers than the sultan in his harem.

Act III, Scene 6, Lines 78–81

Lear (to Edgar): You, sir, I entertain for one of my hundred, only I do not like the fashion of your garments. You will say they are Persian, let them be chang'd.

Note: Persian dress was reputed to be elaborate. Perhaps it reflects Horace's line in *Ode I*, 38, "My boy, I detest Persian pomp," or contemporary travel accounts and the portraits of the Sherley (Shirley) brothers in Persian dress now at Petworth House in England.

THE TRAGEDY OF MACBETH (1606)

Macbeth is the second-shortest play of Shakespeare after *The Comedy of Errors* and nearly half the length of *Hamlet*. The source, as with most of Shakespeare's English history plays, is Holinshed's *Chronicles* on the reign of Duncan King of Scotland (1034–1057). The impetus to Shakespeare's composition according to most scholars is the accession of King James V of Scotland as James I of England on the death of Elizabeth I in 1603. James had extended his patronage to Shakespeare's actors' company and the name was changed from "The Chamberlain's Men" to "The King's Men." Heretofore Shakespeare had not written a play with a Scottish setting. Furthermore, as James I was intensely interested in witchcraft and had written a book, *Demonology* (Edinburgh 1597), Shakespeare inserted the witches and their prophecies.

When the play opens Macbeth is a celebrated commander who has put down an insurrection and hon-
ors are to be bestowed on him by Duncan the king. On
his way to an audience with Duncan he encounters
three witches who prophesy greater things for him. As
each prophecy is fulfilled, Macbeth's ambition grows.
Encouraged and emboldened by his wife, he kills the
king and assumes his throne.

Macbeth is one of the darkest of the great tragedies
of Shakespeare. There is an ominous air pervading the
play from the beginning. It is accentuated by having
all the famous scenes take place at night or in some
dark corner. What weakens the play is that the only
fully drawn characters are Macbeth and Lady Macbeth who appears in only the first half of the play. Lady
Macbeth is the more fully realized and she dominates
her limited scenes. However, Macbeth and Lady Macbeth are not as articulate as other key characters in
Shakespeare. The other principal characters – Duncan
the king, Banquo, Macduff, and Malcolm – are defined
only by broad strokes and we learn little about them.

The play ends with the forces of good triumphant.
Macbeth is killed in battle and Malcolm, the son of
the murdered king, is crowned.

Act I, Scene 3, Lines 4–7

Witch I: A sailor's wife had chestnuts in her lap...

Her husband's to Alepppo gone, master
   o' th' *Tiger*...

Act III, Scene 4, Lines 98–102

Macbeth: What man dare, I dare.

Approach thou like the rugged Russian bear,

The arm'd rhinoceros, or th' Hyrcan tiger,

Take any shape but that, and my firm nerves

Shall never tremble…

Note: Hyrcania was a province of ancient Persia known for its fierce tigers (see note on *The Merchant of Venice*, II, 7, 39–43).

Act IV, Scene 3, Lines 34–37

Macduff: …Fare thee well, lord,

I would not be the villain that thou think'st

For the whole space that's in the tyrant's grasp,

And the rich East to boot.

Act V, Scene 1, Lines 50–51

Lady Macbeth: Here's the smell of the blood still.
All the perfumes of Arabia will not sweeten this
little hand.

THE TRAGEDY OF ANTONY AND CLEOPATRA (1606–07)

The play is based on Plutarch's *Lives*. In addition to the main characters – Antony, Cleopatra, and Octavius Caesar – Shakespeare develops several minor characters from a few references in Plutarch, such as Iras and Charmian, and creates a wholly new engaging character, Enobarbus. The setting of the play is much of the known globe of the day. Cleopatra says of Antony, "His legs bestride the ocean; his rear'd arm crested the world" (V, 2, 82–83).

Antony is not the shrewd Antony of old as he appeared in *Julius Caesar*. He was then a master of political maneuver, an orator who swayed and mesmerized the crowd, albeit by demagoguery, and built a mighty coalition that took revenge on the assassins of Julius Caesar. Now we see him deliriously in love with Cleopatra who has virtually enslaved him. He forgets and ignores his wife Octavia, the sister of Octavius Caesar, who will soon become the sole ruler of Rome. Antony divides his time between Egypt and Rome and cannot wait to return to Egypt: "I shall to Egypt; …I' th' East my pleasure lies" (II, 3, 38–40). His god has become Bacchus and he is half drunk in most scenes. Once clever, he is now outclassed by the wily politician Octavius who has come to detest Antony for having abandoned his wife.

Cleopatra is also madly in love with Antony. She too has abandoned her public responsibilities and yearns for him to come back to Egypt. In a memorable scene she shows her longing for Antony: "O Charmian where think'st thou he is now? Stands he or sits he? Or does he walk or is he on his horse? – O happy the horse, to bear the weight of Antony!" (I, 5, 19–21).

Shakespeare's Cleopatra is one of his great dramatic figures. She is beautiful, intelligent, determined, and wily. Enobarbus describes her thus: "Age cannot wither her, nor custom stale her infinite variety. Other women cloy the appetites they feed, but she makes hungry where most she satisfies" (II, 2, 240–42).

Act I, Scene 2, Lines 100–3

Messenger (to Antony): Labienus –

This is stiff news – hath with his Parthian force

Extended Asia; from Euphrates,

His conquering banner shook, from Syria

To Lydia and to Ionia…

Note: Quintus Labienus who had supported Brutus and Cassius against the triumverate had now secured a force from Orodes, king of Parthia, against Antony and Octavius Caesar. Labienus was commanding a Parthian army and was overrunning the Roman provinces in Asia.

Parthia was a region annexed to the Persian Empire in A.D. 226, at what is now Khorasan province in northeastern Iran. The Parthians freed themselves from the rule of the Seleucids who had followed Alexander's rule and founded the Parthian Empire, which extended from the Euphrates across Afghanistan to India and from the Oxus to the Indian Ocean. Then began a decline of the empire and they were conquered by Ardashir the founder of the Iranian Sasanid dynasty in A.D. 226.

Act II, Scene 3, Lines 32–34, 39–44

Antony: Get thee gone.

Say to Ventidius I would speak with him.

He shall to Parthia…I will to Egypt;

And though I make this marriage for my peace,

I' th' East my pleasure lies.

[Enter Ventidius.]

O come, Ventidius,

You must to Parthia. Your commission's ready;

Follow me and receive'r.

Act III, Scene 1, Lines 1–11, 16–20

[Enter Ventidius as it were in triumph (with Silius and other Romans, Officers, and Soldiers), the dead body of Pacorus borne before him.]

Ventidius: Now, darting Parthia, art thou strook, and now

Pleas'd Fortune does of Marcus Crassus' death

Make me revenger. Bear the King's son's body

Before our army. Thy Pacorus, Orodes,

Pays this for Marcus Crassus.

Silius: Noble Ventidius,

Whilst yet with Parthian blood thy sword is warm,

The fugitive Parthians follow. Spur through Media,

Mesopotamia, and the shelters whither

The routed fly; so thy grand captain, Antony,

Shall set thee on triumphant chariots, and

Put garlands on thy head.

Ventidius: …

Caesar and Antony have ever won

More in their officer than person. Sossius,

One of my place in Syria, his lieutenant,

For quick accumulation of renown,

Which he achiev'd by th' minute, lost his favor…

Note: In the text, "darting Parthia" and the feared "Parthian Shot" refer to their skill in throwing darts and arrows, especially to cover retreats.

Marcus Crassus was a member, with the elder Pompey and Julius Caesar, of the first triumvirate. He was killed by the Parthians under King Orodes after defeating him in 53 B.C.

Media was an ancient country southwest of the Caspian Sea. It was conquered by Cyrus the Great who became king of the Medes and Persians in the mid-seventh century B.C.

Syria was a country repeatedly invaded by Babylon, Egypt, and others. It was a maritime province under the Phoenicians.

Mesopotamia was the land between the Tigris and Euphrates Rivers. The name derives from the Greek for "middle" and "river." It is part of current-day Iraq.

Act III, Scene 2, Line 42

Agrippa: O Antony! O thou Arabian bird!

Note: Arabian bird is the legendary Phoenix, a unique fabulous bird only one of which was said to exist at a time.

Act III, Scene 6, Lines 4–16

Octavius Caesar (speaking of Antony): …

Cleopatra and himself in chains of gold

Were publicly enthron'd…

Unto her

He gave the stablishment of Egypt, made her

Of lower Syria, Cyprus, Lydia,

Absolute queen.

…

His sons [he there] proclaim'd the kings of kings:

Great Media, Parthia, and Armenia

He gave to Alexander; to Ptolomy he assign'd

Syria, Cilicia, and Phoenicia.

Note: Media, Syria – see note on III, 1, lines 1–11.

Parthia – see note on I, 2, lines 100–103.

Act III, Scene 6, Lines 65–76

Caesar: No, my most wronged sister, Cleopatra

Hath nodded him to her. He hath given his empire

Up to a whore, who now are levying

The kings o' th' earth for war. He hath assembled

Bocchus, the King of Lybia; Archelaus

Of Cappadocia; Philadelphos, King

Of Paphlagonia; the Thracian King, Adallas;

King Manchus of Arabia; King of Pont;

Herod of Jewry; Mithridates, King

Of Comagena; Polemon and Amyntas,

The Kings of Mede and Lycaonia,

With a more larger list of sceptres.

Note: Pontus and Lycaonia were ancient countries of southern Asia Minor, at one time ruled by Persia.

Mede – see note on Act III, Scene 1.

Act IV, Scene 14, Lines 62–71

Antony: …Thou art sworn, Eros,

That when the exigent should come…

Disgrace and horror, that on my command

Thou then wouldst kill me…

Eros: The Gods withhold me!

Shall I do that which all the Parthian darts,

Though enemy, lost aim and could not?

Note: Parthian darts – see note on III, 1, lines 1–11.

Act V, Scene 2, Lines 200–202

Dolabella (to Cleopatra): …Caesar through Syria
Intends his journey, and within three days
You with your children will be sent before.

CORIOLANUS (1607–8)

Based on Plutarch, the play is set in Rome in its early republican days. It differs from the later republican period of Julius Caesar when there was talk of an imperial Rome that came into being under Octavius Caesar (the setting for *Antony and Cleopatra*). The Rome of *Coriolanus* is a city state constantly at war with the rival city state of Antium, home of the Volscians. Caius Martius is the celebrated Roman general who saved his republic numerous times and has been honored with the name Coriolanus. He believes he should also be rewarded with the title of consul of Rome. In anger he leaves Rome and joins an invading army, but his love for Rome prevents him from attacking her. In a somewhat contrived ending Coriolanus is murdered by hired assassins. Aufidius, the Volscian general, pays tribute to the fallen Coriolanus.

Shakespeare was a believer in social order and the real villain of the play is the mob for whom Shakespeare had shown his disdain in previous plays. The great character in the play is Volumnia, Coriolanus's mother, one of the most powerful and dominating characters in Shakespeare.

Act IV, Scene 2, Lines 23–25

Volumnia: …I would my son,

Were in Arabia, and thy tribe before him,

His good sword in his hand.

Note: In this context Arabia denotes some desert spot where no one would intervene.

CYMBELINE (1609–10)

The play is partly based on Holinshed's *Chronicles* and set in pre-Christian, semi-legendary Britain. Cymbeline is king of Britain, ruling about the time of Christ. The gods are Roman. There is still warfare with Roman legionaires in Britain. Cymbeline has two sons who had been kidnapped and a lovely temperate daughter Imogen from his first wife. He is now dominated by his wicked and crafty second wife, the reigning queen, who has a son Cloten from her first marriage. Cloten is arrogant and calculating. When Imogen secretly marries Posthumus Leonatus, a noble but impoverished man, Cymbaline, under the influence of the crafty queen who has plotted for Imogen to marry Cloten, turns against his daughter and banishes Posthumus. Cloten attempts to court Imogen but fails.

The queen and her son plot to turn Posthumus and Imogen against each other. At play's end, Imogen and Posthumus are reconciled; the kidnapped sons are united with their father and sister. Cloten disappears and the queen goes mad.

Cymbaline is not regarded as amongst the best of Shakespeare's plays. The characters are thinly sketched, the plot is too convoluted, and there is very little poetry of note.

Act I, Scene 6, Lines 14–21

Jachimo: All of her that is out of door most rich!

If she be furnish'd with a mind so rare,

She is alone th' Arabian bird, and I

Have lost the wager. Boldness be my friend;

Arm me audacity from head to foot,

Or like the Parthian I shall flying fight –

Rather, directly fly.

Note: The Arabian bird is the phoenix. (See note on *Antony and Cleopatra*, III, 2.)

The mounted archers of Parthia shot arrows backwards while retreating. (See note on *Antony and Cleopatra*, III, 1.)

Act III, Scene 4, Lines 33–35

Pisanio: …no 'tis slander,

> Whose edge is sharper than the sword, whose
> tongue outvenoms all the worms of Nile…

Note: **Worms refer to serpents of the Nile River.**

THE WINTER'S TALE (1610–11)

Leontes, king of Sicilia, has invited his boyhood friend Polixenes, king of Bohemia, to his court. The two have so enjoyed the reunion that Leontes asks his friend to extend his visit. As he is unable to persuade Polixenes he asks his wife Queen Hermione to intervene. Hermione succeeds, but Leontes becomes insanely jealous and begins to think she has been unfaithful with Polixenes. His insane jealousy leads him to ask his close advisor Camillo to poison Polixenes. Camillo knowing that the queen and Polixenes are innocent refuses and escapes with Polixenes to Bohemia.

Leontes publicly proclaims the queen an adulteress and imprisons her with her young son, even knowing that the queen is about to have another child. Hermione gives birth to a daughter, Perdita. Leontes orders the child to be taken to a desert and left to die. Perdita is found by a shepherd who raises her as his own. In the meantime, the oracle at Delphi pronounces that Hermione is chaste and the charges against her are baseless. Leontes's obsession and temporary madness has lost him his wife, his daughter, his son, and his trusted advisor. He is now penitent. Most critics believe Leontes suffered from a form of temporary insanity as it terminates as abruptly as it began.

In the second part of the play, Perdita is found; Hermione is well; the bond of friendship between Leontes and Polixenes is restored; Perdita is married to Polixenes's son Florizel; and the trusted counselor Camillo has returned. The title of the play, echoing the line "A sad tale's best for winter" (II, I, 25), refers to the first part. The second part beginning with the discovery of the abandoned baby is a sort of celebration. Perdita is one of the loveliest of Shakespearean creations. The play also deals marginally with the arbitrary and unchecked powers of rulers. In that respect there is a thematic unity with *Measure for Measure*.

Act III, Scene 2, Lines 119–23

(Queen) Hermione: The Emperor of Russia was my father.

O that he were alive, and here beholding

His daughter's trial!

Act V, Scene 1, Lines 163–67

Florizel: Good my lord,

She came from Libya

…My best train

I have from your Sicilian shores dismiss'd;

Who for Bohemia bend, to signify

Not only my success in Libya, sir,

But my arrival, and my wife's, in safety
Here, where we are.

THE TEMPEST (1611)

The last play wholly written by Shakespeare. It is set on a magical island, probably somewhere near the Americas. Shakespeare always made great use of English travelers, the places they had been, and the reports of their voyages. *The Tempest* is set during James I's reign. On 2 June 1609 an expedition of nine ships had set sail from Plymouth for the colony of Jamestown, Virginia, founded two years earlier. On 25 July a storm dispersed the ships. All the vessels reached Jamestown with the exception of the *Sea Adventure* with about 150 aboard, including the governor of the new colony. Somehow the *Sea Adventure* made it to the island of Bermuda where they built new boats and reached Jamestown on 23 May 1610. *The Tempest* was inspired by the voyage of the *Sea Adventure*.

Prospero, the Duke of Milan, has been deposed by his treacherous brother Antonio who usurped the dukedom with the complicity of Alonso, king of Naples, and exiled Prospero and his young daughter Miranda. Gonzalo, a loyal subject, placed enough provisions in their boat for a long journey. Gonzalo also left Prospero his magic wand and his book of magic. After a long journey they reach an idyllic island that had only one inhabitant, Caliban, the savage child of a witch. Prospero uses his book to tame him. Also on the island is a spirit of the winds, Ariel, a most endearing figure who obeys Prospero's magic. Prospero arranges for a boat carrying the king of Naples, his son Ferdinand, his own evil brother Antonio, and their entourage to be stranded on the island. Next Prospero contrives a romance between Ferdinand and his daughter. Their marriage unites the kingdom of Naples with the dukedom of Milan.

The play has some of Shakespeare's most beautiful lines. Prospero: "We are such stuff as dreams are made on, and our little life is rounded by a sleep" (IV, 1, 156–58). Miranda: "O wonder! How many goodly creatures are there here! How beauteous mankind is! O brave new world that has such people in it" (V, 1, 182–85). There is a passage by Prospero that has generally been interpreted as Shakespeare's farewell to the theatre: "I'll break my staff, bury it certain fathoms in the earth, and deeper than did ever plummet sound I'll drown my book" (V, 1, 54–57).

Act II, Scene 1, Lines 69–71

Gonzalo: Methinks our garments are now as fresh as when we put them on first in Africa, at the marriage of the King's fair daughter Claribel to the King of Tunis.

Act II, Scene 1, Lines 83–86

Adrian: …She was of Carthage, not of Tunis.

Gonzalo: This Tunis, sir, was Carthage.

Adrian: Carthage?

Gonzalo: I assure you, Carthage.

Note: Tunis and Carthage were separate cities though not far apart.

Act II, Scene 3, Lines 31–33

Trinculo: …When they will not give a doit to relieve a lame beggar, they will lay out ten to see a dead Indian.

Note: It has been said that the reference may be to the American Indian, as Jamestown had already been founded.

Act III, Scene 3, Lines 21–24

Sebastian: A living drollery. Now I will believe

That there are unicorns; that in Arabia

There is one tree, the phoenix' throne, one phoenix

At this hour reigning there.

Note: Phoenix – see note on *Antony and Cleopatra*, III, 2, 42.

Act V, Scene 1, Lines 206–11

Gonzalo: …O, rejoice

Beyond a common joy, and set it down

With gold on lasting pillars: in one voyage

Did Claribel her husband find at Tunis,

And Ferdinand, her brother, found a wife

Where he himself was lost…

APPENDIX

A SELECTION OF TRANSLATIONS OF
THE WORKS OF SHAKESPEARE IN SEVERAL
EASTERN LANGUAGES

> *Cassius: How many ages hence*
> *Shall our lofty scene be acted over*
> *In states unborn and accents yet unknown!*
>
> *Julius Caesar* III, 1, 111–13

PERSIAN TRANSLATIONS

It is not easy to determine when theatre as we know it had its start and interest and activity in Shakespeare's works began. Iranian culture is rich in poetry and it was inevitable that sooner or later Iranian poets and writers would be drawn to the plays of Shakespeare. Translations vary widely as to accuracy and poetics. Some better-known early samplings follow.

Play	Translator	Date of Translation	Place of Publication	Notes
Othello	Naser al-Molk (Abu al Ghasem Qaragozlou)	circa 1915–26, published posthumously 1965, republished 1985	Tehran	

Abu al Ghasem Qaragozlou, titled Naser al-Molk II (1863–1927), came from a prominent tribal family of western Iran. His grandfather Mohammad Khan Naser al-Molk was a tribal chieftain and well connected to the Qajar court. As minister of foreign affairs he accompanied Naser al-Din Shah on his second trip to Europe. He took his grandson with him and enrolled him at Balliol College, Oxford (1879–82). Abu al Ghasem Khan returned to Iran and subsequently became regent to the underage Ahmad Shah from 1910–14. He then went to Europe where he stayed until the last year of his life. His translation of *Othello* is competent but devoid of poetry. He may have also translated *The Merchant of Venice*, but no known copy exists.

Play	Translator	Date of Translation	Place of Publication	Notes
Julius Caesar	Mohammad Bahador	1925	Tehran or India	Earliest known translation
Masterpieces from Shakespeare	Unattributed exerpts from *Hamlet, Romeo and Juliet and Macbeth*	1928	Tehran	
The Comedy of Errors	Reza Afshar – serialized in the newspaper *Parvaresh*	1929	Rasht	

Reza Afshar (1887–1964) is one of the more interesting personages in twentieth-century Iran. He graduated from the Urumieh American College in Iran in 1904 and went to the U.S. where he stayed more than eight years attending Wooster College in Ohio and Valparaiso University in Indiana. He spent some time in Berlin then returned to Iran circa 1918-19 and was elected a member of parliament. He was appointed governor of Gilan province, later Kerman, and still later Isfahan; minister of roads; founded Iran Air in 1944, pioneering commercial aviation in Iran. Afshar wrote poetry, which led him to translate The Comedy of Errors.

The Merchant of Venice	Ahmad Bahmanyar Kermani (Dehgan)	1937	Tehran	No longer available
Romeo and Juliet (Lailee & Majnoun of the West)	Aziz Bani Sadr	1938	Tehran	
Much Ado About Nothing	Abdol Hoseyn Nusheen	1950	Tehran	

Not a literal or faithful translation. A French translation served as its basis. Probably Nusheen (1901–71), who was an actor and director, had intended to stage the play in Tehran.

Panj Dastan az William Shakespeare (Five Stories from William Shakespeare)	Nozar	1952	Tehran	

Includes: *The Tempest, A Midsummer Night's Dream, The Winter's Tale, Much Ado About Nothing, As You Like It.*

Hamlet	Masoud Farzad	1957		

Probably the most accurate and poetic translation. Farzad was himself a poet of some distinction. It has an excellent preface and a scholarly postscript indicating the hazards a translator faces. *Hamlet* presents a difficult task as it is the longest Shakespeare play. The translation is heavily influenced by J. Dover Wilson's Freudian interpretation *What Happens in Hamlet.* The notes are useful and accurate and Farzad quotes commentaries by noted Western critics and translators. The book had gone into nine printings by 1997.

Macbeth	Abdol Rahim Ahmadi	1957		
Othello	Abdol Hoseyn Nusheen	1961	Tehran	
King Lear	Javad Payman	1963	Tehran	

Reprinted in 1996. An excellent introduction of some eighty-five pages and a solid translation.

Richard III	Reza Baraheni	1963	Tehran	

Othello	Mahmoud Etemadzadeh (Behazin)	1963	Tehran	
Hamlet	Dariush Shahin	1964	Tehran	
Hamlet	Mahmoud Etemadzadeh (Behazin)	1965	Tehran	
Twelfth Night	Ala al-Din Pasargardi	1965	Tehran	
Henry IV, Part I	Bahman Mohases	1967	Tehran	
Richard II	Reza Baraheni	1969	Tehran	
Macbeth	Farangiz Shadman	1972		
Timon of Athens	Reza Moazemi	1972	Tehran	
Hamlet	Ebrahim Yunesi	1972	Tehran	
Twelfth Night	Afzal Vosouqi	1975	Tehran	
Macbeth	Abdal al-Rahim Ahmadi	1975	Tehran	
The Taming of the Shrew	Hoseynqoli Mirza Salour (Emad al-Saltaneh)	First date of publication un-known		Reprinted in Tehran in 1985
Macbeth	Dariush Ashouri	1992		Second printing in 1994
Richard III	Reza Baraheni	1993	Tehran	
With a foreword discussing the historical background. A superior effort.				
The Tempest	Ebrahim Yunesi	1994		
A good introduction to the play with solid background information. A commendable translation of Shakespeare's last play considering the difficulty of the poetry, some of the very best in Shakespeare.				
Romeo and Juliet	Fouad Vaziri	1996		
Accurate but mostly a prose translation.				
The Merchant of Venice	Ala al-Din Pasargardi	1998	Tehran	

Collected Works of Shakespeare	Ala al-Din Pasargardi	1999	Tehran	

Vol.I	Vol.II
Titus Andronicus	All's Well That Ends Well
Love's Labour's Lost	Hamlet
The Comedy of Errors	Measure for Measure
Romeo and Juliet	Troilus and Cressida
Two Gentlemen of Verona	Othello
A Midsummer Night's Dream	King Lear
The Merchant of Venice	Macbeth
The Taming of the Shrew	Antony and Cleopatra
The Merry Wives of Windsor	Timon of Athens
Much Ado About Nothing	Coriolanus
As You Like It	Pericles
Twelfth Night	Cymbeline
Julius Caesar	The Tempest
	The Winter's Tale

Accurate but non-poetic, with a competent introduction.

Sonnets	Mohammad Homayounvash	2001	Tehran	
A Midsummer Night's Dream	Masoud Farzad	No date or place of publication		
As You Like It	Masoud Farzad	No date or place of publication		
All's Well That Ends Well	Sorouri Saheb	No date or place of publication		
The Winter's Tale	Sorouri Saheb	No date or place of publication		
Romeo and Juliet	Gholamali Fekri	No date or place of publication		
Antony and Cleopatra	Mohammad Ali, Islami Nadushan	No date or place of publication		

A very superior effort based on a French translation. There is a learned foreword by the translator with relevant quotes from Plutarch.

TURKISH TRANSLATIONS

The first Shakespeare translations were by Hasan Bedrettin (1850–1901) and Mehmet Rifat (1851–190?). Mehmet Nadir (1854–1927) translated about forty sonnets, two narrative poems, and some plays. After 1900 translations of the works of Shakespeare increased. Abdullah Wevdet (1869–1932) was the most prolific example of these translators: *Hamlet, Julius Caesar* (1904), *Macbeth* (1909), *King Lear* (1912), *Antony and Cleopatra* (1921). Some later Turkish translations follow.

Play	Translator	Date
Julius Caesar	Mehmet Sukru Erden	1930
The Merchant of Venice	Mehmet Sukru Erden	1930
Othello	Dr. Refet	1931
Macbeth	Mehmet Sukru Erden	1931
Twelfth Night	Mehmet Sukru Erden	1932
The Taming of the Shrew	Nurettin Sevin	1934
A Midsummer Night's Dream	Nurettin Sevin	1936
King Lear	Seniha Bedri Goknil	1937
Romeo and Juliet	Mehmet Sukru Erden	1938
Romeo and Juliet	Ilhan Siyam Taner	1938
Romeo and Juliet	Kamuran Gunseli	1938
The Merchant of Venice	Nurettin Sevin	1938
Romeo and Juliet	Ertugrul Ilgin	1939
Othello	Orhan Burian	1940
Hamlet	English Seminar	1941
Coriolanus	Seniha Sami	1942

Julius Caesar	Nurettin Sevin	1942
The Comedy of Errors	Avni Givda	1943
As You Like It	Orhan Burian	1943
As You Like It	English Seminar	1943
Much Ado About Nothing	Hamit Dereli	1944
The Tempest	Haldun Derin	1944
Antony and Cleopatra	Saffet Korkut	1944
Timon of Athens	Orhan Burian	1944
The Two Gentlemen of Verona	Avni Givda	1944
Hamlet	Orhan Burian	1944
A Midsummer Night's Dream	Nurettin Sevin	1944
Romeo and Juliet	Yusuf Mardin	1945
The Merry Wives of Windsor	Haldun Derin	1945
Coriolanus	English Seminar	1945
Richard the Third	Seniha Sami	1946
Antony and Cleopatra	Senia Sami	1946
The Taming of the Shrew	Nurettin Sevin	1946
Richard the Third	Berna Moran	1947
King Henry VIII	Belkis Boyar	1947
Antony and Cleopatra	English Seminar	1949
Troilus and Cressida	S. Eyuboglu, Mina Urgan	1956
King Lear	Irfan Sainbas	1959
Romeo and Juliet	Adli Moran	1959
Macbeth	S. Eyuboglu	1962

Othello	Ulku Taner	1964
Hamlet	S. Eyuboglu	1965
Julius Caesar	S. Eyuboglu	1966
Romeo and Juliet	Turan Oflazoglu	1968
Timon of Athens	S. Eyuboglu	1968

The bases for the above translations fall into four categories: some from a recognized English text; some from French translations; others from German translations; and reworked Turkish translations.

ARABIC TRANSLATIONS

In the late nineteenth century *Othello, Hamlet,* and *Romeo and Juliet* were produced on stage and became known in the Arab world. Some early translators remain anonymous. They did not work directly from Shakespeare's text but mainly from French and some Italian translations, and even took liberties with those. Verse translations of Western plays were very rare up to the 1930s. In the early twentieth century two schools evolved. One favored a literalist approach with faithful translations. The other favored translation of the essential meaning of the text with Arabic equivalents of Shakespeare's images. Among the latter was the noted Egyptian poet Khalil Mutran. The vast majority of Shakespeare translations have been published in Egypt, principally Cairo. Some samplings over the years follow.

Play	Translator	Date	Place of Publication
Romeo and Juliet	Nigula Rizq Allah	1899	Cairo
Hamlet	Amin al-Haddad	1907	Cairo
The Tempest	Muhammad 'Iffat	1909	Cairo
Macbeth	Muhammad 'Iffat	circa 1911	
Othello	Khalil Mutran	1912	Cairo
Julius Caesar	Sami I-Juraidini	circa 1913	Cairo
King Henry V	Muhammad al-Siba'i	circa 1913	
Julius Caesar	Nashid Luqa	circa 1919	
The Merchant of Venice	Khalil Mutran	1922	Cairo
Julius Caesar	Louis Ghannam Thabit	1925	Cairo
Julius Caesar	Khalil Mutran	1927	
King Lear	Khalil Mutran	1927	
The Tempest	Khalil Mutran	1927	
Coriolanus	'Umar 'Abd al-'Aziz Amin	1927	Cairo
The Tempest	Muhammad 'Abd al-'Aziz Amin	1929	Cairo
The Taming of the Shrew	Ibrahim Ramzi	1932	
King Henry V	Sami Juraydini	1936	Egypt
King Henry VIII	'Abd al-Rahman Fahmi	1936	

Antony and Cleopatra	Muhammad 'Awad Ibrahim	1945	Cairo
Twelfth Night	Muhammad 'Awad Ibrahim	circa 1945	
Romeo and Juliet	'Ali Ahmad Bakthir	circa 1946	
King Henry VIII	Muhammad 'Awad Ibrahim	1947	Cairo
Richard II	Mahmud 'Awad Ibrahim	1948	Cairo
Hamlet	Khalil Mutran	1949	Cairo
Hamlet	Kaddur Fattal	1952	
Romeo and Juliet	Ali Ahmad Ba Kathir	1969	Cairo

In the 1970s the Cultural Committee of the Arab League in Cairo recommended sponsoring an authoritative translation of the complete works of Shakespeare. The project was carried out under the general editorship of Taha Husayn, the dean of Arabic letters.

TRANSLATIONS OF SHAKESPEARE IN INDIA

India is a special case. The lengthy British presence in India made an impression on its society. Shakespeare's plays were performed in English and were translated and performed in several of India's indigenous languages over a long period of time. Suffice it to say that they probably have been as numerous and varied as in any Eastern country.

BIBLIOGRAPHY

Ackroyd, Peter. *Shakespeare, The Biography*. New York, 2005.

Adams, John Quincy. *A Life of William Shakespeare*. United States, 1925.

Akrigg, G. P. V. *Shakespeare and the Earl of Southampton*. London, 1968.

Bloom, Harold. *Shakespeare, The Invention of the Human Mind*. New York, 1999.

Bradbrook, M. G. *Shakespeare: The Poet in His World*. London, 1978.

Bradley, A. C. *Shakespearean Tragedy*. London, 1926.

Brown, Ivor. *Shakespeare in His Time*. Great Britain, 1960.

Campbell, John Lord. *Shakespeare's Legal Requirements*. London, 1859.

Cartwright, John. *The Preacher's Travels*. London, 1611.

Chambers, E. K. *William Shakespeare: A Study of Facts and Problems*. 2 volumes. Oxford, 1930.

Chardin, Sir John. *The Travels of Sir John Chardin into Persia*. London, 1691.

Chute, Marchette. *Shakespeare of London*. New York, 1949.

Curry, Walter Clyde. *Shakespeare's Philosophical Patterns*. Baton Rouge, 1937.

Davies, D. W. *Elizabethans Errant: The Strange Fortunes of Sir Thomas Sherley and His Three Sons*. U.S., 1967.

Dover Wilson, J. *Life in Shakespeare's England*. Cambridge University Press, 1926.

———. *What Happens in Hamlet*. Cambridge, 1956.

Ferrier, R. W. *A Journey to Persia: Jean Chardin's Portrait of a Seventeenth Century Empire*, London 1996.

Floor, Willem. *The History of Theater in Iran*. Washington, DC, 2005.

Ghani, Cyrus. *Iran and the West*. Washington, DC 2007.

Greenblatt, Stephen. *Will in the World: How Shakespeare Became Shakespeare*. U.S., 2004.

Halliday, F. E. *The Life of Shakespeare*. Great Britain, 1963.

Harbage, Alfred. *Shakespeare and the Rival Traditions*. New York, 1952.

Harrison, G. B. *Shakespeare under Elizabeth*. New York, 1933.

Herbert, Sir Thomas. *A Relation of Some Years Traveile Begunne Anno 1626 into Afrique and the Greater Part of Asia, Especially the Territories of the Persian Monarchie.* London, 1634.

———.*Some Years Travels into Diverse Parts of Africa and Asia – Particularly the Empires of Persia and Hindustan.* London, 1677.

Hotson, Leslie. *The First Night of Twelfth Night.* London, 1954.

Javadi, Hassan. *Persian Literary Influence on English Literature.* Calcutta, 1983.

Jenkinson, Anthony. *Early Voyages and Travels to Russia and Persia.* Two volumes. London, 1886.

Kermode, Sir Frank. *The Age of Shakespeare.* New York, 2003.

———. *Shakespeare, Spencer, Donne.* London, 1971.

Knight, G. Wilson. *Shakespeare and Religion.* London, 1967.

Lee, Sir Sidney. *A Life of Shakespeare.* London, 1915.

Marco Polo. *The Travels of Marco Polo.* New York, 1939.

Maurois, Andre. *A History of England.* New York, 1958.

Murray, John Middleton. *Shakespeare.* London, 1936.

Olearius, Adam. *The Voyages and Travels of the Ambassadorship of Frederick, Duke of Holstein to the Duke of Muscovy and the King of Persia.* London, 1669.

Plutarch. *Plutarch's Lives*. Translated by John Dryden, revised by Arthur Hugh Clough. New York: Modern Library, no date.

Ross, Sir E. Denison et al. *Anthony Sherley and His Persian Adventures*. London, 1933.

Rowse, A. L. *The Expansion of Elizabethan England*. University of Wisconsin Press, 1955.

———. *Shakespeare's Southampton, Patron of Virginia*. London, 1965.

———. *The Annotated Shakespeare*. Three volumes. New York, 1978.

Savory, Roger. *Iran under the Safavids*. Great Britain, 1980.

Schoenbaum, S. *Shakespeare: The Globe and the World*. U.S., 1979.

Shakespeare, William. *The Complete Plays and Poems*. Edited by Willam Allen Neilson and Charles J. Hill. Cambridge, Massachusetts, 1942.

———. *The Riverside Shakespeare*. Edited by G. Blackmore Evans. Boston 1974.

———. *The Complete Works* (The Pelican Edition). Edited by Stephen Argel and A. R. Braunmuller. New York, 2002.

Shapiro, James. *A Year in the Life of Shakespeare*. New York, 2005.

Spurgeon, Caroline. *Shakespeare's Imagery and What It Tells Us*. Boston, 1958.

Trevelyan, G. M. *A Shortened History of England*. Great Britain, 1974.

Uruch Beg. *Don Juan of Persia: A Shia Catholic,
1560–1640.* Translated by O. G. Le Strange. Great
Britain, 1926.

Williams, Neville. *The Tudors.* Edited by Antonia Fraser.
California, 2000.

Wood, Michael. *Shakespeare.* U.S., 2003.

ARTICLES

Bernard, Philippa. "Rodrigo Lopez: Physician to the
Queen." Lecture given at Westminster Synagogue,
London, 17 February 1981.

Draper, John W. "Shakespeare and Abbas the Great."
Philological Quarterly 30 (4 October 1951): 419–25.

Morgan, Wm Gerry. "Shakespeare's Knowledge of
Medicine." Lecture delivered before the College of
Physicians of Philadelphia, 10 March 1930: 307–22.

Savory, Roger. "The Sherley Myth." *Iran V* (1967): 6–7.

BOOKS AND ARTICLES IN PERSIAN

Bayzai, Bahram. *Namayesh dar Iran* (Theater in Iran).
Tehran, 1383 (2004).

Falsafi, Nasrallah. *Zendegi Shah Abbas* (The Life of Shah
Abbas I). Five volumes, sixth printing, Tehran, 1375
(1996).

Khaleqi Motlaq. "Iran in the Pre-Islamic Era." *Iran Shenasi*, fourth year, no. 2 (summer 1992): 240–41.

Ma'ki, Ebrahim. *Shenakht Avamel Namayesh* (Recognition of Principles of Theater). Tehran, 1363 (1984).

Matini, Dr. Jalal. "Iran in the Islamic Era." *Iran Shenasi,* fourth year, no. 2 (summer 1992): 243–98.

Navai, Dr. Abdol Hoseyn. *Iran va Jahan; As Moghul ta Qajar* (Iran and the world; from Mongol invasion to Qajars). Tehran, 1377 (1998).

Navai, Dr. Abdol Hoseyn and Ghaffarifard, Dr. Abbas Qoli. *Tarikh Siasi, Eqtesadi va Farhangi dar Iran dar Dowran Safavi* (The History of the Political, Economic and Cultural Movements in Iran During the Safavid Era). Tehran, 1381 (2002).

Sotoodeh, Dr. Manuchehr with the cooperation of Iraj Afshar. *Asnad Padrian Carmeli: Bazmandeh Az Asr Shah Abbas Safavi* (Documents Pertaining to Carmelite Fathers from the Shah Abbas I Era). Tehran, 1383 (2004).

INDEX

A

Abbas II (Shah) 44, 46
Abbas (Shah) 35, 38, 39,
    45, 46, 48, 61, 62, 114,
    179, 180
Abdallah Khan Ustajlu 56
Abu Bakr 35
Ackroyd, Peter 64, 65, 91,
    175
Adams, John Quincy 2,
    175
Aeschylus 29
Albuquerque, Alfonso
    de 52, 54
Alexander (The Great) xiv,
    29, 30, 120, 132, 151, 154
Ali (descendent of Shaykh
    Safi) 34
Ali Ibn Abu Talib 35
Alikhani, Alinaghi x
Ali Qoli Beq 86

Anne Boleyn 16, 17
Anne of Cleves 17
Arden, Mary 3
Ardeshir I 30
Ashraf (Afghan ruler) 45
Ataturk. *See* Mostafa Kamal
    (Ataturk)
Augustine (Saint) 50

B

Barbaro, Josafa 52
Bernard, Philippa 71, 179
Bloom, Harold 74, 175
Bolingbroke (Henry
    IV) 72, 74, 123, 124, 125
Bradley, A. C. 91, 175
Browne, Edward G. 47

C

Cabot, John 54
Cabot, Sebastian 54, 55

G

Galileo 44
Gengis Khan. *See* Changis
  Khan
Ghani, Caroline x
Ghani, Dr. Ghasem 47
Godunov, Boris 82
Goethe 12, 138
Greene, Robert 2, 7

H

Hafez 12
Hakluyt, Richard 54
Hall, Dr. John 11
Hall, Elizabeth 11
Harbage, Alfred ix, 176
Harrison, G. B. 90, 176
Hathaway, Anne 4
Hathaway, Richard 4
Hatton, Sir Christopher 21
Haydar (Safavid) 34
Heminges, John 2
Henry III of Castille 51
Henry IV 72, 123, 126,
  129, 131
Henry of Navarre 76, 77
Henry Tudor 13, 14
Henry V 10, 13, 126, 129,
  131
Henry VI 13, 14, 118
Henry VII 13, 14, 15, 16,
  122
Henry VIII 3, 8, 15, 17, 18,
  19, 24, 68, 134, 173
Henry VI, Part III 15

Herbert, George 81
Herbert, Thomas 59
Hormozd (King) xiv
Hoseyn Ali Beq Bayat 84
Howard, Catherine 17

I

Isabella (Queen) 15
Isama'il I (Shah) 35, 37,
  45, 47
Isma'il II (Shah) 39
Ivan IV (The Terrible) 55

J

James I 26, 66, 74, 75, 84,
  85, 87, 104, 147, 161
James VI 83
Jane Grey 19
Jane Seymour 17, 18
Javadi, Hassan 51, 62, 177
Jenkinson, Anthony 55,
  56, 57
John of Gaunt 9, 13, 26,
  123
Johnson, Richard 55
Johnson, Robert 55
Jonson, Ben 1

K

Kamshad, Hasan x
Karpivicz, Dolmet 57
Katz, Jeff ix
Kepler 44
Kermode, Sir Frank 71, 73,
  135, 177

SOME OTHER MAGE TITLES

My Favorite Films
Cyrus Ghani

A Man of Many Worlds
The Diaries and Memoirs of Dr. Ghasem Ghani
Cyrus Ghani / Paul Sprachman

Iran and the West
Volumes I & II
Cyrus Ghani

The Strangling of Persia
Morgan Shuster

The Persian Revolution of 1905–1909
Edward G. Browne / Introduction by Abbas Amanat

The History of Theater in Iran
Willem Floor

Agriculture in Qajar Iran
Willem Floor

Crowning Anguish: Taj Al-Saltana
Memoirs of a Persian Princess
Introduction by Abbas Amanat / Translated by Anna Vanzan

New Food of Life: Ancient Persian and
Modern Iranian Cooking and Ceremonies
Najmieh Batmanglij

From Persia to Napa: Wine at the Persian Table
Najmieh Batmanglij

Silk Road Cooking: A Vegetarian Journey
Najmieh Batmanglij

Happy Nowruz: Cooking with Children to Celebrate
the Persian New Year
Najmieh Batmanglij

Stories from the Shahnameh of Ferdowsi
The Lion and the Throne, I
Fathers and Sons, II
Sunset of Empire, III
Translated by Dick Davis

Vis and Ramin
Fakhraddin Gorgani / Translated by Dick Davis

Borrowed Ware: Medieval Persian Epigrams
Translated by Dick Davis

My Uncle Napoleon
Iraj Pezeshkzad / Translated by Dick Davis

Inside Iran: Women's Lives
Jane Howard

The Persian Sphinx:
Amir Abbas Hoveyda and the Iranian Revolution
Abbas Milani

Tales of Two Cities: A Persian Memoir
Abbas Milani

The Art of Persian Music
Jean During / Zia Mirabdolbaghi / Dariush Safvat

The Persian Garden: Echoes of Paradise
Mehdi Khansari / M. R. Moghtader / Minouch Yavari

Masters and Masterpieces of Iranian Cinema
Hamid Dabashi

Stories from Iran: A Chicago Anthology 1921-1991
Edited by Heshmat Moayyad

Savushun: A Novel about Modern Iran
Simin Daneshvar / Translated by M.R. Ghanoonparvar